The Majestic Quran
A Summary of the 30 Chapters

The Majestic Quran

A Summary of the 30 Chapters

by Musharraf Hussain

The Majestic Quran - A Summary of the 30 Chapters

First edition published February 2021

INVITATION PUBLISHING,
512-514 Berridge Road West
Nottingham
NG7 5JU

Distributed by
INVITATION PUBLISHING
Tel: +44[0] 115 855 0961
E-mail: info@invitationpublishing.co.uk

Copyright © Invitation Publishing 2021

All rights reserved. No part of this publication may be reproduced stored in a retrieval system, or transmitted in any form or by any means, electronic, mechanical, photocopying, recording, or otherwise, without the prior permission of the copyright owner.

Cataloguing-in-Publication Data is available from the British Library.

ISBN: 9781902248905
Typeset in Minion Pro.
Front cover: Hagia Sophia Holy Grand Mosque, Turkey
Printed in Turkey by: Imak Offset.

Contents

Foreword 8
Introduction 9

Juz 1	11	Juz 16	75
Juz 2	15	Juz 17	79
Juz 3	19	Juz 18	83
Juz 4	25	Juz 19	87
Juz 5	31	Juz 20	93
Juz 6	35	Juz 21	97
Juz 7	39	Juz 22	101
Juz 8	43	Juz 23	105
Juz 9	47	Juz 24	109
Juz 10	51	Juz 25	113
Juz 11	55	Juz 26	119
Juz 12	59	Juz 27	125
Juz 13	63	Juz 28	131
Juz 14	67	Juz 29	137
Juz 15	71	Juz 30	143

Foreword

Beautifully succinct, this summary extracts the main themes and lessons of the Quran in clear, concise, and flowing English, making it easily accessible to the reader. Having a daily connection with the Quran is essential in our lives, it brings light and tranquillity to the hearts. In addition to pondering over the ayaat of the Quran, being able to see the themes weaving through the Quran, enables us to reflect upon the central ideas that Allah Almighty is drawing our attention to.

In Dr Musharraf Hussain's summary we can see how the rich tapestry of the Quran moves seamlessly between stories of previous nations, key ayaat, and rulings on how to navigate our lives and the Quran's questions that challenge us to think. The inclusion of the dates of the historical events behind the revelation give us insight into the context surrounding the section and the Surah.

I commend Dr Musharraf on completing this wonderful piece of work, which will enable readers to have an overview of the Quran. May Allah reward him for his efforts and accept them.

> — Shaykh Haytham Tamim is the founder and teacher at the Utrujj Foundation. He has an unbroken chain of scholarship, which goes back the Prophet ﷺ. Shaykh Haytham Tamim serves on various boards and panels and is the leader of the Lebanese Sunni community in the UK under Dar Al-Fatwa (UK).

February 2021

Introduction

Reading The Majestic Quran means different things to different people. From childhood we have been conditioned to tilawat, the recitation of the Quran for the sake of sawab, Divine reward; that's great, but let me add that you should read the English translation too, study the Quran with your mind and experience the life-changing message of Allah's book. It will improve your spiritual health, your character and bring you closer to family and friends. The reading of the Quran in English will give you spiritual energy and boost your physical, psychological and spiritual well-being. Here is your daily Quran reading plan during Ramadan.

The feel-good challenge: Read the Majestic Quran every day
This summary of each Juz can be read in less than 10 minutes. By setting the goal of reading the whole of the Quran this Ramadan for yourself, you will get encouragement to learn and understand and achieve satisfaction at the end. Without learning new things, you cannot grow. So, start today by reading the Majestic Quran, and with Allah's help work towards it every day.

Put aside 10 minutes daily for the English reading of this summary. Then ask yourself: what is the Quran saying to me? How can I live according to this teaching? How will I monitor my progress? Do this for the whole Ramadan.

Recitation of the Quran during Ramadan is Sunnah
One night during the month of Ramadan, the Prophet, stayed in the masjid after the 'isha prayer and performed additional salah. Some sahabah (companions) joined him. The next night he did the same accompanied by more sahabah and the third night saw an even greater number. However, on the fourth night he left the

masjid immediately after praying the fardh prayer. The next night he did the same when asked about this he said, "I don't want to burden my followers." He told the Sahaba, "I read the whole of the Quran in Ramadan with Jibreel". It was this Sunnah that prompted the early Muslims to adopt the practice of reading the complete Quran in the month of Ramadan. To facilitate this the Quran was divided into 30 equal parts. Each part is called Juz (Plural Ajza).

When Umar ؓ became khalifah, he saw large numbers of people staying behind after isha', praying individually. After consulting scholarly sahabah, he established the tarawih prayer as a regular congregational prayer during Ramadan. He instructed that it should be lead by a competent hafiz (person who has memorised the Qur'an), and a Juz of the Quran should be read each night. So everyone would be able to listen to the entire Quran at least once a year.

The congregational Tarawih is now performed as 20 rakahs of salah, performed two units at a time with a rest period between every four rakahs, which was originally used for making tawaf (circumambulation) of the Kabah in Makkah and performance dhikr in Madinah. Some masjids organise speakers for these times, while others perform a group dua'.

Juz 1

الم

Surat Al-Fatihah [1] - The Opening

In the name of Allah, the Kind, the Caring.

All praises are for Allah the Lord of the worlds. The Kind, the Caring. The Controller of Judgement Day. We worship You alone and from You alone we seek help. Guide us on the straight path: the path of those You favoured, not those who are condemned or the misguided ones.

Surat Al-Baqarah [2] - The Cow

The first Juz opens with the Surat Al-Baqarah revealed over two years in Madinah after the migration of the Prophet ﷺ in 622 CE (Common Era). By now two-thirds of the Quran had been revealed in Makkah during a tense situation. In Madinah, Muslims faced new challenges: settling down in a new city with Arabs and Jews. The two Arab tribes, the Aus and the Khazraj, both with a long history of rivalry. There were three Jewish tribes, they had moved to Madinah after they were expelled from Jerusalem by the Romans. The Jews were literate, skilled and affluent compared to the Arabs and believed they were "the chosen people".

The Surat opens by describing the people of Madinah and dividing them into three groups: the believers, the disbelievers and the hypocrites. The Faithful are described as having firm belief in Allah, the unseen realities and the Hereafter; they pray regularly and give charity generously. The disbelievers have locked minds unwilling to listen. Then follows a section listing the evil habits of hypocrites: deceivers and liars, who mock the believers and make trouble, they are ignorant, misguided, and disorientated.

Worship is a way of being thankful to the Lord who created and sustains and cares for humanity. Those who worship him will have Paradise, an amazing reward.

The creation of Adam and Eve, the first humans, is narrated and Adam is designated the lofty title of Khalifa, the Divine representative on earth. Angels were ordered to prostrate before him, but Satan refused and was expelled from Paradise. Adam is honoured by Allah and educated about all the things in the universe. When he and his wife Eve mistakenly eat from the forbidden tree, they are expelled from paradise and sent down to earth.

The story of the Jews (40-141) dominates the rest of the first Juz. The Jews are the children of prophet Yaqub, the grandson of Ibrahim. Allah reminds them of His favours: a special contract with them gave them faith, law and scripture. They are reminded how Allah saved them from the slavery of Pharaoh. Unfortunately, they did not all fully appreciate this and were ungrateful. Despite their betrayal, Allah blessed them with Manna, and Salva, delicious pre-cooked meat and dessert respectively.

In the middle of the Juz is the story of the cow, from which the Surat takes its name. A man was murdered, but an innocent person sentenced to death. Musa told them to stop the execution, and to investigate the truth. They were to sacrifice a cow and swipe the dead body with it, as they did so, the murdered person rose from the dead and identified the murderer. As a commentary on the story, the Quran laments about people who after seeing such miracles still refused to believe in resurrection. What is the relevance of this story in a Surat that lays down many laws? To point out that human society is not based on laws only, but civil society must respect moral and social values and spiritual ideals. A legal system is only one part of a flourishing civilisation. The Story of the Cow highlights the idea that attitudes and values lie at the heart of a just society.

Over the next few sections, the Quran pours scorn on the Israelites for breaking the contract, killing prophets and being arrogantly stubborn. They are reminded that they disrespected the Angels, Jibreel and Mikeel, and prophet Sulayman. They accused Sulayman of magic and Allah exonerated him from such fraudulent practices.

The Messenger ﷺ eagerly preached and invited the Jews of Madinah to accept Islam. However, their religious pride, tribal jealousy and economic prowess stopped them. Furthermore, their love of this world blinded them from seeing the truth, it points out their blind pursuit for worldly power. By recalling their worldliness and carefree attitude to Allah the Muslims are being warned to take note.

The supreme status of the Messenger ﷺ is highlighted in the passage by teaching believers how to address him properly. They are invited to become one community and stop the sectarian bickering. After making sincere and powerful arguments to embrace Islam, the Quran categorically says people are free to worship as they like (114). The vastness of Allah's creation is proof of His existence; the disbeliever's rejection does not diminish His Glory.

Jewish history began three thousand years ago with their great grandfather Ibrahim. It opens with his prayer for his descendants who he settled in Makkah. The prayer for a Messenger to be raised among them. An Allusion to the Beloved Messenger Muhammad ﷺ. So, why don't you accept him? Ibrahim's faith was deep, and he had a long-term vision for his children including his children from Ismaeel too. Before ending the story of the Jews, Yaqoob's final advise to his twelve sons is mentioned, "They say to you: "Become Jews…", or: "Become Christians and you will be guided". Tell them:

"In fact, our religion is the religion of Ibrahim, who was a true Hanif, and was not an idolater". Say: "We believe in Allah and in what is revealed to us, and in what was revealed to Ibrahim …" (2: 139).

These sections describe the unity of the Abrahamic faiths by pointing out that Islam is not a new religion, but verifies, confirms and continues the teachings of Judaism and Christianity. They too accept the belief in one God and of serving humanity. Islam replaces Judaism and Christianity as the final religion of Allah, so the Quran is The Final Revelation.

Juz 2

سَيَقُولُ

Surat Al-Baqarah [2] continued

In Madinah, the Muslims were free to practice Islam in a way they were not able to in Makkah. They are encouraged to develop a civil society defined by a belief system with spiritual and moral values and underscored by legal and political standards. The Surat established a clear legal context to support this spiritual and moral social structure and to tackle the sickness of an uncaring society. In addition, political and economic principles were laid down including:

- The change of the direction of prayer from Jerusalem to Makkah (142). This signalled the end of the hegemony of the Jewish people. It heralded the new dawn of Islam; commitment to Allah and service of humanity as a mark of distinction. Furthermore, there is the motivation for everyone to set goals and direction for their lives. This requires patience and spiritual help from Allah.
- The four forbidden foods (172); pork, blood, carcasses and animals slaughtered without invoking Allah's name.
- When questions on alcohol, gambling, charity and shortchanging orphans were asked, the Quran disapproved such behaviour.
- Fasting in Ramadan is made obligatory (183).
- Muslims are given permission to fight against others in defence (190).

- The morals and manners of Hajj and Umrah are explained (197).
- Family laws; the law of retribution (178); writing down one's will (180); the prohibition of marriage with non-Muslims (222); divorce and marital discord (228-32).
- Entering Paradise or Hell may be determined by who one marries.
- An answer to a question about menstruation and sexual intimacy.
- The ruling about settling marital disputes.
- The rights and responsibilities of married couples and divorcees.
- Third-time divorce.
- Avoiding injustice when going through a divorce.
- A father has to pay maintenance expenses for his children.
- The waiting period for widows, and encouragement to remarry.
- Divorce ruling before the marriage is consummated.
- Never neglect your prayers under any circumstances.
- Further rulings on maintenance for widows and divorcees.
- Commercial transactions; the prohibition of earning interest (275); business contracts; commercial transactions and guarantees for loans (282-283).

Salvation lies in submission to Allah

An overview of Juz 2 reveals an important thread that weaves it together "Human salvation lies in complete submission and commitment to the Lord of the Worlds". This is comprised of the following five principles:

1. Firm faith in Allah, the One God.
2. Belief in his Majestic rule and Power.
3. Belief in Allah as the sole creator of the Universe.
4. Belief in His messengers who have been sent to guide humanity and to make clear the straight path that will help creation to achieve the pleasure of the Creator.

5. Belief in life after death.

Such beliefs help us to live a righteous life, a good life pleasing to the Lord and conducive to healthy living and well-being. This is not a mechanical performance of ritual exercises. Instead, it is conscious awareness of and attentiveness to the Divine, in such a way that one feels His presence everywhere. A natural outcome of this way of living is the belief in a resurrection and Judgement Day, signifying that this life is an opportunity to gain the pleasure of Allah, and therefore to secure a place near Him in Paradise.

Diversity among various faiths and ways of living

The Quran presents diversity in creation as "Allah's way" and nothing unusual or strange about it. Say, "We believe in Allah and what is revealed to us, and what was revealed to Ibrahim, Ismael, Ishaq, Yaqub and the tribes, as well as what was given to Musa and Isa, and what was given to all the Messengers from their Lord, we make no distinction between any one of them, we are Muslims" (136).

Some key questions

The new community in Madinah faced many challenges, which were addressed through the following questions:
- How should Muslims relate to the Jews in Madinah?
- What is Ibrahim to Muslims? Ibrahim's prayer for Prophet Muhammad ﷺ was: "Our Lord raise among them a noble messenger, who will recite your verses unto them and teach them the Book and the Wisdom, and will purify them; you are the Almighty, the Wise" (129). In other words, the religion of Islam is the fulfilment of the prayer of Prophet Ibrahim.
- Should Muslims take up arms against the enemy?
- Fighting is compulsory for you although you dislike it. Sometimes you dislike something that is good for you and sometimes you like something that is bad for you. Only Allah knows the truth, but you do not know (216).

- The Muslims were given permission for the first time to take up arms against the enemy to defend themselves. This contrasted with the policy in Makkah, where they could not physically retaliate against aggression.
- What is the nature of a Muslim's relationship with Allah? "When My servants ask you about Me, tell them I am near; I answer the prayer of the prayerful whenever he prays to Me. Therefore, obey Me and believe in Me so that you may be guided" (186).

As we reach the end of the Juz, the Surat returns to the story of the Israelites, the sacred Ark, which contained the relics of Musa and Harun was used by them as a centre of spiritual energy through which they won against their enemies. They are reminded how they sought a king and Allah gave them Talut and later Dawud.

Juz 3

تِلْكَ ٱلرُّسُلُ

Surat Al-Baqarah [2] continued

The opening verse of this Juz points to the spiritual hierarchy, prophets are honoured according to their ranks. This supported the Israelites idea of 'being favoured people'. However, Allah sets the rule of meritocracy, and that is based on faith, efforts and Divine grace. The 'Verse of the Throne' is a glorious portrayal of Allah's majesty, power and control of the universe, its message is that all humans can attain Allah's friendship and nearness through virtuous deeds.

Freedom of religion is a recurrent theme of the Quran
"There is no compulsion in religion. Guidance is clearly distinct from error. Whoever rejects false gods and believes solely in Allah has grasped the most trustworthy handhold, which will never break. Allah is the All-Hearing, the All-Knowing" (256).

The theme of Allah's friendship of the believers continues and examples are given of how He cared for His friends:
- Ibrahim defeats the tyrant Emperor Namrood.
- Uzair is shown Allah's power over life and death.
- Ibrahim witnesses the resurrection of dead birds.

The attitudes and behaviours of the friends of Allah are characterised by generosity. They are willing to spend in the way of Allah what they have. Parables are told to show their virtue in glowing terms:
- Parable of a single grain teaches that giving one pound will earn seven hundred pounds.

- The parable of the soil-covered rock teaches the message to not be shallow and mean when giving, but to give freely without seeking favours in return.
- Whether you give openly or secretly, do it to please Allah.
- Recognise the genuinely needy, find a worthy cause to support.

Allah declares war on people who take usury, charging extortionate rates of interest on loans. Usury contradicts human nature, which is to be compassionate as opposed to taking advantage of the poor and exploiting them.

- All commercial deals should be recorded and written in the presence of witnesses.
- The place of securities and trust in business deals. Witnesses are required to protect those liable.

After so many legal orders the reader is reminded that this comes from Allah, who has knowledge of all things visible and invisible, so bear him in mind all the time, you are being watched! The Surat ends by giving details of the beliefs of faithful, just as it opened by describing their qualities. Finally, it closes with a prayer of reassurance and seeking Divine kindness.

Surat Ale-'Imran [3] - The Family of Imran

The third Juz continues with Surat Ale-'Imran, revealed after the battle of Uhud, in the Shawwal of 3 AH (Anno Hegirae, "in the year of the Hijra"). It tells the story of 'The family of Imran,' the father of Maryam, the mother of Prophet Isa.

The Quran is the absolute standard for goodness, the Surat opens by proclaiming that Allah's revelation has been continuous from the beginning of time and that it includes the Torah of the Jewish Scriptures, the scrolls revealed to many other prophets and the Gospels of the Christians. The Quran is a continuation of that chain and the final revelation. So, the People of the Book are invited to embrace this final testament.

Searching for the hidden meanings of the Quran could mislead. So, the Quran warns against focusing on ambiguous and metaphorical passages and making arbitrary interpretations that go against the spirit of the divine message, thus sowing the seeds of conflict, even though, "Only Allah knows their exact meaning" (7). This kind of 'stretching' the meanings of divine scripture was the root of sectarianism rampant among the Jews and Christians. The Christian doctrine of the divinity of Jesus and the declaration that Jesus is the 'son of God' is an example of this arbitrary interpretation of the Gospel.

Worldly wealth and power aren't a guarantee of success
The defeat of the Makkans in the Battle of Badr had confirmed this reality. The worldly wealth and luxuries are fleeting and temporary whilst the fruits of righteous life will be everlasting in paradise. This is a result of submission to Allah, a deep commitment to serving the Lord. This is true religion, the guidance and way forward. So, those who are disobedient will be punished. But the committed servants of the Lord solemnly pray: "Allah, Master of all power, You give power to anyone You will and you take it away from anyone You will."

How do we demonstrate this commitment to Allah? "Say, if you really love Allah and have committed to Him then follow me, He will love you and forgive your sins" (31)

After explaining the nature of Islam, submission and commitment an example is given of a family who did this, the family of Imran.

The story of Maryam
The story of Maryam's childhood is beautifully told through the miracles that occurred around her. When Prophet Zakariyya her carer saw them, he prayed. Allah blessed him with a son, Yahya. This is followed by an account of Maryam's virgin conception and

the birth of Isa. Maryam is praised as the one 'chosen above all the women of her time'.

Maryam grows up in the holy sanctuary. She will be the mother of a great prophet, Isa. When Jibreel tells her that she will conceive 'the spirit of Allah' she's scared. But she's reassured of Allah's blessings. Isa grew up and preached Tawhid, some followed him while others rejected him. Isa calls his disciples, and they confirm they are Muslims.

Since the Christians claimed that his miraculous birth and the miracles were proofs that he is God, the Quran explained the special nature of Isa and challenged their erroneous doctrine of Trinity. It asserted that "Isa is like Adam; [Allah] created him from dust then said to him 'Be!' and he was" (59).

Even though Judaism, Christianity and Islam differ in their respective beliefs they are still told to sit and talk. This plea encourages peaceful coexistence: "people of the book, let's agree on a common statement that exists between us: we worship no one except Allah" (64). To prove the commonality of the three faiths the Quran stated: "Ibrahim was neither a Jew nor a Christian since the Torah and the Gospels were revealed much later. The three faiths are invited to follow him. This is a Quranic approach to reconciliation.

The next two passages invite both Jews and Christians to stop misleading people by clever arguments and tricks, they are no substitute for Divine guidance. They are warned against changing Allah's words or their meanings. The Quran gives an acid test about belief in Allah, how can the prophet who was sent by Allah, ever demand that he should be worshipped? This is absurd. To prove the unity of all prophets and their singular message of Tawhid, the Quran presents an account of the conference of the prophets, when they were asked "if another messenger comes to you confirming what you have, then you must believe in him and lend him your support... they all agreed" (81).

Islam means submission to Allah, which is the only true religion. It was established by Ibrahim, preached by Musa and Isa. It is the same message Muhammed is inviting you to. Faith determines our eternal salvation, faith must be clearly understood, in words and terms that are plainly clear without any ambiguity, so the Quran cautions "lookout for words and actions that lead to apostasy" (86-91).

Juz 4

$$\text{لَنْ تَنَالُوْ الْبِرَّ}$$

Surat Ale-'Imran [3] continued

The fourth Juz opens with the declaration, you will only do well when you give your best. Learn lessons from the stories of the Israelites. Muslims do not invent beliefs and practices that contradict divine teachings nor innovate. Before declaring the pilgrimage as an obligation for anyone who can afford it, the Quran gives the background of the Kaaba, in Makkah, as the first place of worship built on Earth.

   A warning is given not to deny Allah's favours. Among them, the Unity of the believers, a sense of belonging to good people. The Ansar of Madinah are reminded of their bloody and bitter past. Sectarianism is condemned, examples from the Jewish infighting are given to stress the destructive nature of disunity. The uniting power of Islam calls Muslim to play a leading role in inviting humanity to goodness and rejecting evil. This is the special calling of Muslims. If they ignore it they will be disgraced.

   Despite these criticisms of the Israelites, the Quran cautions against stereotyping people due to religion and race. Allah said: "All of them are not alike; a group among the People of the Book upholds the original teachings of the scripture, reciting Allah's verses throughout the night as they prostrate to Him… Whatever good they do, it will never go unrewarded by Allah, Allah knows the pious." (113-115).

   This is followed by two sections full of pearls of wisdom, such as:
- Virtuous deeds without faith in Allah are worthless

- Friends should be chosen wisely

The story of the Battle of Uhud (121-177)
The next fifty-six verses tell the story of the battle of Uhud. Since the Makkans defeat at the Battle of Badr, they were determined to avenge their dead. So they gathered an army of 3,000 men to attack Madinah. When the Prophet ﷺ learnt of this, he held a war council. The overwhelming opinion was to go out of the city and meet the enemy in the open field. The Muslims numbered about 700.

The Messenger ﷺ strategically posted fifty archers on the nearby hill, to provide cover against outflanking manoeuvres by the enemy cavalry. They were to stay there under all circumstances. However, when they saw Muslims winning the battle, they left their post and scrambled for the booty. Seeing this opportunity, the Makkan cavalry, veered round in a wide arc and attacked the Muslims from the rear. This unexpected attack resulted in the loss of many lives. Amidst all this mayhem. A rumour quickly spread that the Prophet ﷺ had been killed and this caused some Muslims to flee. However, Omar and some other companions dispelled the rumour and regrouped to defend the Prophet ﷺ. When the other Muslims learnt that the Prophet was alive, they rallied and attacked the enemy. The Quraysh fled to Makkah. The battle ended as a draw and seventy Muslims were martyred.

Hard lessons learnt from the Battle of Uhud
This was a devastating blow due to sloppy discipline and disobedience of the Prophet. The lesson was "Obey your leader." The Quran provided a detailed analysis of what went wrong: "When you were defeating them with His help, suddenly you lost courage, argued about the order you had been given and disobeyed it, even after He had shown you what you desired – the fact is that some of you long for the world, whilst others among you long for the Hereafter" (152). A harsh criticism, but Allah reassures the

Muslims, "Do not be disheartened or sad, you will come out on top if you are true believers" (139).

The next sections highlight the reasons for this defeat and the lessons, which must be learnt:
1. The archers' anguish about missing out on the spoils of war. Wars must never be fought for gaining booty.
2. During times of trial 'always stand firmly and never despair'.
3. Never disobey the Prophet's order.
4. Be courageous and overcome your doubts.
5. The defeat in the battle distinguished the hypocrites from the believers.
6. The 70 martyrs are with their Lord, enjoying bliss in paradise.
7. Always put your trust in Allah and get on with the job in hand.

Despite the devastating blow to the morale and reputation of the Muslims, the archers were pardoned by Allah. Consolation follows: "Allah favoured the believers when He sent them a messenger. The hypocrites were happy at the defeat of Muslims, they were warned of a dreadful punishment awaiting them. The conclusion is "tests are a part of a life of faith" and you must be patient to succeed (185).

The opening of the Surat tells 'those firmly grounded in knowledge' will believe in the Quran without a doubt. These same people are praised in the last ten verses for being reflective and prayerful. The Lord will answer their prayers. What is true success? It isn't material achievements nor military prowess. "Believers, be patient, encourage each other to be patient, be disciplined, and be mindful of Allah so that you may achieve success" (200).

Surat An-Nisa [4] - The Women

The fourth Juz continues with Surat An-Nisa, revealed over eighteen months after the Battle of Uhud, in 3 AH/625 CE. A third of the Surat discusses family issues. Since seventy Muslim men were martyred, they left behind them orphans and widows, creating families in crisis. There was a dire need for clear guidance on how to deal with this crisis. The Surat lays out a series of laws concerning: the status of women, marriage, marital discord, inheritance, capital punishment for murder, the prohibition of praying under the influence of alcohol and the rights of orphans. It provides instructions on settling family disputes arising out of what is nowadays called "post-traumatic stress disorder". It lays out clear rulings to ensure justice is done, but still emphasizes the need to be caring and loving towards orphans and one's family. In this way, a safe space is created for the nurturing of children.

The Surat opens by stressing the need to maintain family ties, as they connect us to each other. The key to this is fairness and taking care of those who are most vulnerable. The seventy martyrs of Uhud had left behind orphans and widows so it was important to give them legal protection. Trustees of these orphans were advised to look after their property wisely and not to squander it. Similarly, the law of inheritance was announced: different shares for different relatives: the male heirs share is double that of the female. This was revolutionary legislation since it was unheard of giving women inheritance. The inheritance is distributed after the deceased's debts have been paid and any bequest fulfilled. The maximum amount of bequest allowed is a third of the inheritance. The parent's share is one-sixth; wife's one quarter if there are no children, if there are children then it's one eighth. The Quran stresses the reward for adhering to Allah's boundaries and not violating Divine commandments.

The peace and prosperity of family life depends on the chastity of the spouses so the Quran lays down serious penalties for adultery; an evil that can destroy the harmony and success of family life.

Is repentance acceptable? Yes "However, if they repent and reform themselves, then leave them alone. Allah is the Relenting, Most Kind." The next three sections outline the women that a man cannot marry and thereby ends some terrible unjust customs of pre-Islamic Arabia. The list of women forbidden as spouses: mothers; daughters; sisters; maternal aunts; paternal aunts; nieces from the brother's or sister's side; foster mothers who have suckled you, foster sisters; your mothers-in-law; the stepdaughters who are in your care from women with whom you have consummated marriage; the wives of your sons; and marrying two sisters at the same time (23).

Juz 5

وَٱلْمُحْصَنَاتُ

Surat An-Nisa [4] continued

The fifth Juz opens by declaring that a man and woman can enjoy intimacy and loving relationship only through marriage. Marriage is the most cherished relationship and the dowry symbolises its importance. Only marry a believing woman, the Quran declares. Marriage is a wonderful institution where two people share pleasures and sorrows. The ingredient for a successful marriage is honesty.

Inheritance
Be content with your share of the deceased's estate. Do not wish for more. Verse 34 answers the awkward question – why the unequal shares for men and women? Because men are obliged to spend on their wives, they have a bigger share in the inheritance and they must work to support the family.

Despite marriage being a loving relationship, things will go wrong, so how do you heal marital conflict? The Quran suggests 'Mediation' is the way. Whilst discussing family issues we are reminded about the purpose of religion: worship Allah…be kind to parents, relatives, orphans, needy, neighbours, and travellers.

Verses 44 to 57 describe some of the problems Muslims were having with the Jews of Madinah. The Quran laments about the growing jealousy and resentment and advises everyone to obey the law and the authority.

Obedience to the Messenger ﷺ is a source of blessing
Good leadership is a powerful glue that holds a society together, "Believers, obey Allah, the Messenger ﷺ and those in authority amongst you, if you disagree amongst yourselves over anything, then refer it to Allah and the Messenger" (59). A later verse gives a further reason why the leadership of the Prophet ﷺ was so important, explaining that, "We haven't sent a single messenger for any purpose except he should be obeyed by the will of Allah. If only, when they wronged themselves, they were to come to you and seek Allah's forgiveness and the Messenger too would seek forgiveness for them" (64). Those who obey the Messenger ﷺ are blessed: "Whoever obeys Allah and the Messenger, these are the one Allah has favoured, like the Prophets, the truthful, the martyrs and the righteous. What wonderful companions!" (69).

Jihad isn't for worldly gains
Verses 71 to 80 condemn Jihad for worldly gains and stress its purpose is to fight injustice and there is no escape from death when the time comes.

Tackling Hypocrisy
Verses 81 to 91 highlight the problems caused by the Hypocrites, a notorious group who were neither with the Muslims nor openly against them, they were the fifth column who always found excuses to avoid following the Shariah. The Muslims are told to ignore them and don't worry about their rumours. The way to counter hypocrisy is, to be honest, sincere and genuine to oneself. To care and serve others, particularly members of one's family and to show love and respect for the leadership of the community and always be courteous. These guidelines will shape a peaceful, harmonious and just society. The penalty for accidental homicide and murder (92-93). Murder incurs the death penalty and Allah's anger.

The Quran wants to develop the character of its followers, so it is peppered with pearls of wisdom: "do not be judgmental or dismissive, instead be open, honest and transparent." This is about the Muslims who couldn't emigrate from Makkah. Do not be judgmental about strangers you meet, only Allah knows the true state of people's hearts and minds. However, this does not pardon those who could have migrated but didn't. There is a tacit encouragement to emigrate from a place where you can't live according to your faith.

The next section: "When you are travelling in the land, you can shorten the prayer without any guilt" (121). This dispensation is followed by a simple way of praying when in a state of fear or battle. Even in such danger, the prayer cannot be overlooked. To avoid Hell, Muslims must follow the path of Allah's pleasure and they should not expect the Messenger ﷺ to follow their whims. If he were to follow them there would be chaos and injustice. A severe warning is given "Whoever opposes the Messenger after the guidance has been made clear and follows a path other than that of the believers, We will let him continue down his chosen path until We throw him in Hell" (115).

The Satan tricks people by giving false hopes, spreading weird customs, misleading Allah's creation by encouraging them to associate false gods with Allah. The Quran teaches: "Allah will not forgive idolatry, but He forgives whatever is less than that" (116). However, Satan's tactics are weak. People who Submit wholeheartedly to Islam can resist his misguidance. They are behaving like the rest of the natural world, which submits to Him, and so, "they will be admitted to gardens beneath which rivers flow, remaining there forever, Allah's true promise" (122).

The next section revisits Safeguarding of orphans and the right of women to inherit. The order is to 'be just'. Women are advised to seek help when facing marital disputes. "Reconciliation is the best policy, but humans tend to be selfish. So, remain righteous and mindful, Allah is aware of what you do" (128).

Attention is drawn to the glory of Allah, as everything belongs to Him: "Whoever desires the reward of this world only, then let him know that the reward of this world and of the Hereafter are with Allah. Allah is All-Hearing, All-Seeing" (134).

Standing up for Justice
When these radical laws about inheritance were announced, there was a backlash from the supporters of the old customs, so the Quran inspired people to Stand up for justice and struggle against prejudice. "Believers, stand up for fairness as Allah's witnesses even if it's against yourselves, parents or relatives, and regardless of whether a person is wealthy or poor" (135).

The hypocrites were the masked ones, the two-faced cowards prowling around spreading mischief. They sat on the fence for the victor to emerge, before they declared faith. They are told it will be an eternal waiting. They tried to deceive Allah Almighty; they made a show of praying, the Muslims are warned against taking them as allies as they cannot be trusted.

Juz 6

لَا يُحِبُّ ٱللهُ

Surat An-Nisa [4] continued

If someone is treated unfairly, they can disclose the wrongdoers' identity. An important principle of religion is 'it's all or none'. You cannot choose to do one thing and leave out another, it is a complete submission or complete rejection, no half-way!

Next is the story of the Prophet Isa and how the Jews betrayed him. It also criticises the Christians for manufacturing stories around his crucifixion, resurrection and divinity. The Quran is categorical about Isa not being killed. He was raised alive to heaven and will return near the end of time. Despite this criticism of the Jews and Christians we are reminded not to stereotype, they are not all alike: some are guided and others misguided.

The process of revelation was the same for all the prophets, so Isa was no different from the rest of the prophets. So, why do you regard Isa as the son of God? "Those who deny the truth and stop others from the path of Allah have wandered far" (169).

People are warned; Do not be fanatics nor stretch the meaning of the gospels in a way that contradicts Isa's teachings. Their beliefs, that he died for the sins of humanity, the trinity and that he was the son of God, are all false. Why do they think that Isa would be embarrassed to be called the servant of Allah? The Prophet Muhammed ﷺ was great in many ways, but he was proud to be called 'the servant of Allah'. He is the Messenger ﷺ a clear proof of Allah's Majesty. So, those who believe in Allah and hold firmly to their belief in Him, will be treated kindly with His grace, and He will guide them towards Himself along a straight path.

More on inheritance; those who die childless: if they had a sister, she would inherit half; If there are two sisters, they inherit two thirds (176).

Surat Al-Ma'idah [5] - The Feast

This chapter was revealed in Madinah after the Treaty of Hudaibiya, except verse 3, "Today I have completed your religion for you …" which was revealed at the Farewell Hajj 10AH/631CE. The period after the Treaty of Hudaibiya marked a new era in the history of Muslims. Now they were free to preach and propagate Islam in the Arabian Peninsula, as agreed in the treaty. The economic prowess of the Jewish tribes had now waned and the Muslims were confident and optimistic.

Allah's contract with Muslims is laid out. It puts it in the context of the contracts the Jews and Christians had with God. They broke the law, invented false beliefs and changed some of the laws in the Torah and the Gospel. So, they were dismissed from the privilege of the favoured people of Allah. Muslims are warned, abide by the Shariah to earn Allah's favour. Allah prefers those who obey the law.

The new Muslim state needed laws to function as a well-ordered civil society. In this Surat, eighteen new laws are decreed: contracts; testimony and the importance of honest witnesses; respecting sacred months; slaughtering animals; the lawfulness of seafood; rules of entering into a state of ihram for pilgrimage; intermarriage with Jewish and Christian women; apostasy; rules for cleanliness; the penalty for stealing; the penalty for brigandage and sedition; prohibition of intoxicants and gambling; atonement for breaking an oath; hunting whilst in a state of ihram; making a will at the time of death; and the penalty for those who violate divine laws.

They are set in the context of various historical events. For example, the story of the Israelites' refusal to obey Musa when told to enter the Holy Land. The lesson is disobeying Allah's messengers deserves punishment; the story of the murder of Abel by Cain, an abominable crime. The relationships of various groups in the Arabian Peninsula are surveyed, and the Christian-Muslim relationship is highlighted: "You will find the nearest and most affectionate to the believers are …the Christians' (82).

Cooperate and don't hate
Muslims are reminded that do not let others past wrongs stop you from being cooperative. Let bygones be bygones. Hatred is a bad policy.

The next section forbids certain kinds of meat: "carrion; blood; pork; whatever is slaughtered in a name other than Allah's; animals killed by strangulation, a blow to the body, fallen from a height, gored; eaten by beasts of prey– unless you are able to slaughter it before it dies – and anything slaughtered on the altars of idols" (3). Animals caught by hunting Dogs and trained birds of prey are halal.

Extramarital affairs are forbidden, to be pure, get married. Muslims are permitted to marry Jewish and Christian women; don't engage in sex outside of marriage, nor have love affairs.

The five daily prayers are obligatory before the prayer perform the ritual washing of Wudu. Justice is important for building social cohesion and harmony. Behave justly, give up discrimination: "Believers, be committed to Allah as witnesses for fairness, and do not let the hatred of a community stop you from being just" (8).

The Israelites contract is revisited, some kept the contract, others neglected it. So, they are invited to follow the way of the blessed Prophet to amend their past wrongs. Particularly the Christian doctrine of Trinity, "Those who say, "The Messiah son of Maryam is God," are denying the truth" (17).

The punishment for those who start a war is the death penalty
The next section is an invitation to get closer to Allah through mindfulness, good company, the search for a spiritual teacher and ways of doing good. This only comes from righteousness, not wealth. Another Divine law to promote justice: eye for an eye is just, but to pardon is charity.

Religious differences are by Allah's will
"For every community in the past, We established law and a way of life. Had Allah wanted, He would have made you one nation, but He chose to test you regarding what He gave you; so, compete in doing good works. You will all return to Allah in the end, and He will inform you regarding your differences" (48). A warning against choosing sides out of fear and not being just, remember Victory is for the lovers of Allah, a harsh warning is given to those who give up their faith, they will ruin themselves. Similarly, a warning is given to those who poke fun at the religious practices of others. "When you call to the prayer, they treat it as a joke and game since they don't understand" (59). They're warned: "they will suffer the curse and anger of Allah and will become like monkeys, pigs and the worshippers of false gods" (60). Christians are invited to give up Trinity so they may achieve salvation.

Juz 7

وَإِذَا سَمِعُوا

Surat Al-Ma'idah [5] continued

The Juz opens with a tribute to Monotheistic and Godly Christians who upon hearing the Quran are moved and accept it's message. Some people had a habit of asking too many questions, they are warned not to do so, as they could be narrowing their own choices and would regret later. This is followed by a penalty for breaking an oath, feed ten needy persons.

Wine and intoxicants like it (including recreational drugs) and gambling are made unlawful since they sow enmity and hatred between people (90). It is interesting that the revelation gives the reason behind the ban, evidence that the Quranic laws are reasonable and in the interest of society.

What is the role of the Messenger ﷺ ?
Deliver the message, not to coerce, nor to convert people, to believe or to reject; Islam cherishes the principle of 'no compulsion in religion' (101).

The Arabs were steeped in superstitions like, piercing the ears of their she-camels and dedicating them to the Idols. They had irrational beliefs in the supernatural influences of these practices believing that they could bring good or bad luck. So, they are told, "rid yourselves of the superstitions of the past generations".

The next section deals with the appointment of witnesses to one's will and end of life directives to prevent conflict among the heirs in the future (106).

The subject of Prophet Isa ﷺ and Christians is revisited. The miracles of Prophet Isa ﷺ: he blew into clay birds and they would fly; healed the blind and the lepers and raised the dead from their graves; fed large crowds (114). The Human nature of Isa and the significance of his prophethood are stressed. Those who saw his miracles misunderstood and regarded him as God. But in the Hereafter Isa will declare his innocence of this blasphemy (118).

Surat Al-An'am [6] - The Cattle

The second part of the 7th Juz begins with this late Makkan Surat, revealed on a single occasion in full. This was a time of severe tensions between the Muslims and the idolaters. Ibn Abbas said that some Makkans told the Prophet ﷺ, "We shall not believe until you bring us a book which we can see, touch and accompanied by the angels who bear witness that it's from Allah and that you are His messenger." The Quran told him that even if they were to touch it with their hands, they wouldn't believe.

Powerful arguments are presented to support beliefs of Tawhid, Risalah, and Akhirah. The title Al-An'am, "the Cattle" is derived from several references to the idolaters' superstitious practices of dedicating animals to their idols. A verse praising the creative power of Allah opens the Surat and criticises them for equating idols with Him. The only remedy for this stubbornness is submission to Sublime Lord. The Quran is a book of guidance a reminder of Judgement Day.

The Oneness of Allah is self-evident, yet the disbelievers refuse to see it, they fail to appreciate the gifts they have. Their eyes will open on the day of Judgement, they'll make excuses but to no avail! "If you could see them on Judgement Day when they stand staring at the Fire; they will say, "If only we could be returned and, instead of denying our Lord's signs, become believers" (27). They were fooled by worldly life, they didn't see "This worldly life is a sport and an amusement, but the home of the Hereafter is far better for the mindful. Don't you understand?" (32).

The Messenger ﷺ was concerned about their fate, but they in return, they taunted and mocked him, so he is consoled and urged to be patient. They say, "If a sign were to come down to him from his Lord?" Say, "Allah has the power to send down a sign," but most of them have no knowledge (37).

The next four passages teach humility: to understand one's true worth, to help readers get this message the Quran uses examples. Humility is seen in animals that live in communities "There is no creature on land or a bird flying in the sky that does not belong to a community like yours" (38).

The blessed Messenger ﷺ is reassured that the arrogance of the idolaters is disastrous. The safest policy is to be humble. Patience in tough times makes you humble as does the company of righteous people. Finally, rely on Allah and acknowledge His greatness. Many previous communities suffered since they ignored the message. But Allah gave them a breathing space: "We opened up the floodgates of everything for them and as they were enjoying what they were given, We seized them and left them in despair" (44).

An example of humility is the Messenger ﷺ himself, he made no extravagant claims for himself. The Prophet ﷺ is equipped to respond to the hostile disbelievers "Say, "I am forbidden to worship those you serve besides Allah." Say, "I won't follow your desires because, if I did so, I would go astray and fail to be guided" (56).

The Evidence of Allah's control over nature: How the soul travels in sleep, His knowledge of the unseen. To protect your faith, avoid gatherings where Islam is criticised and bad mouthed, do not mix with those who plot against Allah's religion. They have adopted playful ways but you must have nothing to do with them. From here onward historical evidence for Allah's Grandeur is provided: Ibrahim's faith is an example. When he saw the splendour of the Heavens and the Earth, the stars, the moon and the sun rising and setting, he asked – who had created them? Ibrahim was rewarded for his unwavering faith and devoutness. He was the father of many prophets. Fifteen Prophets from his line are mentioned in the Quran.

The next section provides powerful evidence for the resurrection: "They failed to recognise the true greatness of Allah when they said, 'Allah did not reveal anything to humanity'" (91). The disbelievers in death throes will regret it, but it will be too late. "Let out your souls, today you will be rewarded with the punishment of contempt because of what you falsely said about Allah, arrogantly rejecting His signs" (93). All are reminded they were born alone and will return alone.

More evidence for the creative power of Allah is given: "We produce pods with seeds packed together and from the flowering part of palm trees, low-hanging clusters of dates, and orchards of vines, olives and pomegranates, some alike and others different. Look at their fruits as they grow and ripen; there are signs in that for people who believe" (99). He is the Originator of the universe. "He created everything, and He knows everything. Such is Allah, your Lord; there is no god but Him, the Creator of everything, so worship Him. He governs everything. Our eyes cannot perceive Him, but He perceives what our eyes see. He is the Subtle, the Aware" (103).

After declaring the Divine Majesty, the Quran instructs: don't insult or mock the beliefs of non-believers. The Quran predicts that these people will not believe even if they were to witness miracles, so do not fret for them! "Most of them are ignorant".

Juz 8

وَلَوْ أَنَّنَا

Surat Al-An'am [6] continued

How the devil misleads?
The idea of believing in one God was too much for the people of Makkah. They thought the Prophet ﷺ was mad. But it was their leaders, referred to as the human devils who were misguided. Allah tells the Messenger ﷺ not to pay attention to their criticism since their world view was distorted by superstitious practices. These superstitions show their cowardly nature. For example, they wouldn't eat meat on which the name of Allah had been invoked. Why do they do these evil things? Evil works look attractive: "Take for example a dead person who We resurrected and gave him a light to walk among people, can he be like someone who lives in darkness which he never leaves? (122).

This simile explains "The person Allah wishes to guide, He opens his mind to surrender to Allah, and whomever He lets go astray, his mind is closed as if he were struggling to climb skywards: by such means, Allah allows evil to come about on those who do not believe" (124). What influenced the sinners? The lure of the world and its delights.

Pagan superstitions about livestock: they fixed shares for idols and Allah. These misinformed superstitions aren't benign but lead to serious sins including infanticide. Allah's creative power; "He grows gardens, both with and without trellises, date palms, plants of different tastes, olives and pomegranates, some alike and others different. Eat of their fruits when they are ripe, give the needy their due on harvest day, and do not squander; He dislikes spendthrifts" (141).

The next section mentions the four pairs of domestic animals: camel, cow, sheep and goat. Allah created them for transport and food. The idolaters are misled and unreasonable.

The oneness of Allah is evident in nature, human history, conscience, self-evident truths and human interest. The result of this belief in Oneness of Allah is people become devout, honest and well-wishers of humanity. This goodness is summarized in the Ten Commandments.

The ten Commandments are the new contract: reject idolatry: care for parents: don't kill children: never be indecent; Don't kill; don't misappropriate orphans' property; be honest in weights and measures; be just; fulfil Allah's contract; follow the straight path, and be responsible representatives of Allah.

The purpose of Allah's revelation is to remove doubts, so why don't you accept the new contract?

The Quran appeals to common sense and repeatedly invites people to see the reality: "You have nothing to do with those who divided their religion and made sects; their case rests with Allah, and He will inform them about what they did." The Prophet ﷺ is told to make his case decisively by announcing "My prayers, my sacrifices, my life, my death; are for Allah, Lord of all the realms. (162).

Surat Al-A'raf [7] - The Heights

Juz 8 continues with this late Makkan Surat which opens by describing the role of the Quran: guidance and a reminder. Otherwise, the consequences would be devastating. The story of Adam reveals the cause of human failure to follow the path of religion. Satan the arch enemy misleads them. So, we are alerted to his plots. His tools are deception that makes things appear attractive and humans readily fall into his trap. He appeals to the psychological hunger, lust, food, sense of belonging and honour. Satan did this with our father and mother Adam and Eve. He tempted them, and they fell into his trap but they quickly repented.

Dressing smartly can be a defence against indecency and arrogance. By linking clothing with piety, the Quran teaches the relationship of the outer to the inner, the physical to the spiritual, and the connection between words and behaviour.

The Quran is a warning and an authoritative reminder like earlier books. But the Makkans denied it. It instructs them to be righteous to earn reward and reserve a place in Paradise. In the Hereafter, all deeds will be weighed. The Quran persuades everyone to achieve it. But the Satan vows to mislead people, he succeeds with many. Satan said, "I shall wait by their straight path for a chance to lure them; then I will pounce on them from the front, their behind, and from their right and left, You will find most of them are ungrateful to You"(14-17).

How did he trap Adam and Eve? He whispered to the two of them, revealing their nakedness, of which they had until then been unaware"(18). This was the result of following his whisper. However, they quickly recognised their mistake and repented. "Our Lord, we've wronged ourselves. If You don't forgive us and treat us kindly, we'll be the losers" (23).

Modesty and the dress code The covering up of the private parts stops lewdness and reduces attracting the attention of the opposite sex. The Quran recommends dressing well and insists, "Children of Adam, we've revealed to you the idea of clothing for adornment and to cover your nakedness, but the clothing of piety is best of all. (26). So, modesty and shame help to escape Satan's temptations. To dress smartly is piety (29-32).

To show the impact of modesty on human salvation the Quran rules: "My Lord has forbidden acts of indecency, whether openly or in secret; likewise any sin; unlawful rebellion; associating with

Allah anything for which He has revealed no authority and saying things that you have no knowledge about Allah" (33).

Shirk is associating idols with Allah and is a serious sin. It deserves harsh punishment. Each successive generation of disbelievers will blame the other. "Whenever a community enters the Fire, it will curse its fellow community, up until each of them has followed all the others into it, and the last of them will say about the first of them, "Our Lord, here are those who misled us, so double their punishment in the Fire" (38).

After describing the scary fate of the people of Hell, the Quran turns to the righteous who recognised the gifts of Allah and worshipped Him. They shall live in Paradise!

The following sections describe the wretched state of the people of Hell; they plead for water to quench their thirst, but their request is declined. No one can help them, the idols they worshipped won't benefit today.

How can you avoid this horrible state? Be humble in prayer to the Lord Who created the universe and work for peace on earth (56).

The last part of Juz 8 tells the human history of disobedience: the stories of the prophet Nuh عليه السلام, Saleh عليه السلام, Hud عليه السلام, Lut عليه السلام, Shu'ayb عليه السلام and Musa عليه السلام. The people of Nuh ignored his sincere advice (59-64); The people of Hud rebelled (65-72); the arrogance of people of 'Ad lead them to disobey Salih (73-79); The people of the Prophet Lut عليه السلام rejected him as too puritanical (80-84); Prophet Shu'ayb عليه السلام stopped his people cheating (85-87).

These stories are invitations to Islam and provided reassurance for the Messenger ﷺ and his followers. These Prophets were rejected, condemned, and some killed. But they continued teaching, preaching and mentoring the people. Finally, divine punishment destroyed them. This is a clear warning to the people of Makkah that if you do not accept my beloved Messenger ﷺ you will face the same fate.

Juz 9

قَالَ ٱلْمَلَأُ

Surat Al-A'raf[7] continued

Prophet Shu'ayb ﷺ who lived in Madyan, east of Sinai faced rejection and persecution: the arrogant leaders of his community said, "We will expel you from our town, Shu'ayb, you and all those who believe in you, unless you return to our way of worship." Eventually, "they were seized by an earthquake so violent that they ended up lying face down in their homes" (91).

The Quran laments "had they become believers they would have been blessed" (97). The more one ignores the guidance the harder it becomes to believe, they become stubborn and arrogant.

From here the amazing story of Musa is told as he faces the rage of Pharaoh. "We sent Musa with our miracles to Pharaoh and his leaders, but they rejected them" (103). Musa asked, "let the Israelites go with me". Pharaoh refuses to listen, despite seeing the miracle of Musa's staff turning to a snake and his palm shining brighter than the sun. Instead, he challenges him to have a contest with his magicians. When the contest takes place and the magicians are confronted with the truth, they give in to Musa's miracle and became Muslims. Pharaoh ordered that they are killed. They prayed "Our Lord, give us patience, and let us die in total submission to You" (126).

Pharaoh then threatens to punish the Israelites if they attempt to escape. Musa encourages them to be hopeful and patient. Eventually, Musa leads them out of Egypt. It is not too long before the Israelites forget the favour and make an outrageous demand

"Musa, let us have a god-like their gods." Of course, he is disgusted with their attitude.

Musa goes to Mount Sinai to speak with Allah. "We kept Musa on mount Sinai … for forty nights". Meanwhile, they made a calf as a god. When Musa returned from Sinai he was appalled by their behaviour. The Quran explains their problem as arrogance that blinds people to the blessings of Allah's guidance, "because they denied Our signs and paid no attention to them" (146).

"Then Musa chose seventy men from his people to meet Allah" (155). These elders demanded to see Allah literally, so they were struck with lightening for their rudeness that killed them. Musa prays for forgiveness; "Decree for us in this world what is good and in the Hereafter; we return in humility to serve you" (156). So they were resurrected.

After witnessing this disobedience, you wonder what does a man of faith look like? All we have seen is rebellion and rejection of the truth. Well, read this description of the people of Allah, the blessed ones: "those who believe him, honour him, support him, and obey the light that was sent with him, they shall be successful." The beloved Mohammed is told to declare his universal message: "Say, People, I am the Messenger to you all from Allah, the sovereignty of the heavens and the Earth belongs to Him; He is the only God, He gives life and death. So, believe in Allah and His Messenger."

After this digression, we again pick up the story of Musa where it was left, in Sinai. They needed water so each of the twelve tribes was given a fountain to drink from. Later, some of them settled on the shores of the Red sea and were commanded not to work on the Sabbath. Saturday was reserved for worship and rest. But they broke the Sabbath law; "When they disrespectfully continued doing what they were forbidden, We said, 'Become like apes, despised!'" (166).

Further punishment was that they would be scattered around the world: "Let there arise against the wrongdoers, people who will inflict the terrible torment on them from now until Judgement Day." A fact of Jewish history. A warning to Muslims too, if you disobey Allah, you will face the same.

The nature of humanity is Divine, made by Allah with the potential of recognising and believing the Creator. "Remember when Your Lord brought out the children of Adam from their sides and made them witnesses of each other. He said, 'Am I not your Lord?' They said, 'Yes, we bear witness.' This is so you will not be able to say on Judgement Day that we were unaware of this contract" (172). This was the first assembly of human souls; the pledge of loyalty.

Temptations are a problem that we find difficult to fight. The story of Ballam ibn Baur demonstrates this. He was a scholarly follower of Musa, who became arrogant and contested Musa; "If We wanted We could have raised his status because of it, but he inclined to lower things and followed his whims" (171).

The Quran gives an unusual example of the deniers, it likens them to a panting dog. "Anyone Allah guides is truly guided but anyone He allows to go astray; such people are the losers" (178). In order to avoid a wretched fate, we are cautioned to reflect and recite the beautiful names of Allah.

The reality of idolatry, of associating anything with the mighty Lord is highlighted as an injustice.

"Do they have legs to walk? Do they have hands to hold? Do they have eyes to see? Do they have ears to hear?" Satan is the main mastermind of idolatry, but the pious avoid being trapped by Satan: by seeking Allah's refuge. He is Hearing, Knowing." They are good listeners, who pay attention to the Quran.

Surat Al-Anfal [8] - The spoils of war

This Surat was revealed after the Battle of Badr, which took place in Ramadan in the second year of Hijra (624 CE). The new Muslim community in Madinah was growing rapidly, both in numbers and economic strength, under the brilliant leadership of the Messenger ﷺ. This growing prowess in the new community made the hypocrites and also the Jews feel threatened. The Makkans too were uncomfortable, for they knew that their trade route to Syria might be blocked.

Juz 10

وَٱعْلَمُوٓاْ

Surat Al-Anfal [8] continued

A moving account of the battle of Badr shows the way the battlefield was organised. The Prophet ﷺ marked the places where some of the Makkan leaders would fall and die. Allah made the enemy appear fewer than they were, and the Muslims appeared to be more than they really were. There was a need to be steadfast and brave on the battlefield. This was to be achieved by being united rather than quarrelling. In a battle, the fighters are ordered to fight bravely but strategically. In addition to this discipline of the Muslim army, Allah sent angels to fight on their side.

Lessons from the battle of Badr
1. The spoils of war must be distributed; one fifth for the Messenger ﷺ to distribute as he likes and four-fifth to be distributed among the warriors.
2. If the enemy plays tricks, then do likewise to counter the plot.
3. Be fully prepared for battle, but work for peace. "However, if they incline towards peace, you incline towards it, and put your trust in Allah" (59-61).
4. True faith can give the believers the strength to face twice as many enemies. "your hundred steadfast men can defeat two hundred" (66).
5. Fighting in Allah's way shouldn't be for worldly gains. "It is not fitting for a prophet to take captives until he has won on the battlefield. Believers, you want what this world offers, but Allah desires the Hereafter for you" (67).

Due to their excellent performance on the battlefield, the Muslims were praised: "The first believers who emigrated and struggled with their wealth and lives in Allah's way, and those who offered them refuge and support, they are each other's protectors" (73).

Surat Al-Tawbah [9] - The Repentance

This Surat was revealed in 9 AH (630 CE) following the successful campaign of Tabuk, 560 kilometres northwest of Madinah. The cancellation of treaties with idolaters was announced during Hajj in the same year. This Surat is set with the background of a looming battle and therefore has an angry tone. This explains why it doesn't begin with the Basmala, "In the name of Allah, the Kind, the Caring".

Historical background to the campaign of Tabuk
After the Conquest of Makkah in 8 AH (629 CE), the influence of Islam in the Arabian Peninsula spread rapidly, and many Arab tribes embraced Islam. The Messenger ﷺ sent letters to the rulers of neighbouring countries, inviting them to Islam. These powers began to take notice of this religious and socio-political change. Until now, foreign powers had shown little interest in the Arabs. Now the Romans were nervous and planned to attack Madinah. So, the Messenger ﷺ, after consultation, decided to launch a pre-emptive attack. Muslims gave generously, and a 30,000 strong army was mobilized. However, the Romans remained in their forts. The Muslims stayed twenty days in that area, and made trips along the southeastern border to win allies and sign treaties with local rulers. This increased Muslim influence considerably in the area.

Say, "If your fathers, children, brothers, spouses, relatives and the wealth you have gathered, the business whose downturn you fear and the houses that delight you, if these things are dearer to you than Allah, His Messenger and struggling in His path, then you should wait for Allah's Judgement to come to pass" (Al-Tawbah:

23). The important event with which this Surat begins is the immediate cancellation of treaties with those Arab idolaters who had repeatedly breached them (1-29).

For the second Hajj, after the Conquest of Makkah, the Messenger ﷺ dispatched a delegation under the leadership of Abu Bakr who made this announcement: "From now on the Kaaba will be in the custody of Muslims; idolaters are no longer its keepers." This implied that the Muslims were now the rulers of the Arabian Peninsula.

A lesson from the Messenger's ﷺ migration from Makkah "If you won't help him, Allah has already helped him when the disbelievers expelled him from Makkah. He was one of the two in the cave when he said to his companion, "Do not worry. Allah is with us." So, Allah sent His stillness over him and helped him with armies that you didn't see, and He foiled their plan, Allah's plan is supreme. Allah is Almighty, Wise. Abu Bakr was the companion who accompanied him on this momentous migration.

The wretched character of the hypocrites is vividly described in verses 38-93. They make excuses, have evil motives, and criticise and insult the Messenger ﷺ and the Muslims. They spread rumours, blaspheme and are miserly. They are a lazy bunch, who love only the worldly life and they constantly lie and break promises. Human beings who have such wretched characteristics cannot be trusted. They pose a real threat to the welfare and security of society. They are the enemy within. Their presence in Madinah was so damaging that the Prophet ﷺ was told to take a very harsh position against them: he denounced them and expelled them from his Masjid. When they built a mosque, he was told to demolish it because they wanted to "divide Muslims and to build an outpost to fight Allah and His Messenger" (107).

Right in the middle of the discussion on hypocrites the Surat digresses and instructs believers to give charity, presenting a powerful antidote to the disease of hypocrisy.

"Zakah is for the poor, the needy, its administrators, people whose hearts and minds are to be won, freeing the slaves, helping people in debt, to advance Allah's cause, and for the needy traveller. This is a duty instructed by Allah, and Allah is the Knower, Wise" (60).

Juz 11

يَعْتَذِرُونَ

Surat Al-Tawbah [9] continued

The goodness of the faithful
Whilst Surat Al-Tawbah exposes the wicked nature of the hypocrites, it honoured the true believers as Allah's property, "Repentant, worshippers, praise Allah, fast, bow, prostrate, enjoin good, forbid evil, and keep to the boundaries of Allah" (112). The loyal and dedicated companions are praised, "Allah is well pleased with them, and they are pleased with Him and He has prepared for them gardens with running streams where they will live forever; that is the greatest victory" (100).

The story of the three sincere Muslims who remained behind during the campaign of Tabuk. When the Prophet ﷺ returned from Tabuk, he reprimanded them and no one was to speak to them for forty days. But eventually, they were forgiven. The Surat takes its name, Al-Tawbah, from Allah's acceptance of their repentance.

After congratulating the true Muslims on what they have achieved, the Surat urges them to take the education of religion seriously: "A group from each community should stay behind to thoroughly understand the religion and warn their people when they return to them, so they shall be mindful (122)."

One cannot fail to notice a striking contrast between the opening passage of the Surat and its ending. The beginning shows Allah's anger towards the disbelievers who breached treaties and the wretched hypocrites, while the ending shows kindness and the loving nature of the beloved Messenger ﷺ. In some ways explaining the paradox of war and peace, the harshness of the battlefield is a reality of life if its purpose is to establish justice and remove human suffering.

Surat Yunus [10] - The Prophet Yunus ﷺ

This is a late Makkan Surat, revealed a year or so before the Hijrah in 622 CE. This is the first of the six Surats named after a prophet. The others are Hud ﷺ, Yusuf ﷺ, Ibrahim ﷺ, Muhammad ﷺ and Nuh ﷺ. The Surat opens by asking why people are surprised that Allah sent the revelation to a human being. It continues, with the praise of Allah as the Creator of the universe and explains that the sun, the moon, and the established daily cycles of night and day on earth have been created with a purpose.

The central theme is the truthfulness of the glorious Quran. The Makkans demanded that the Quran be changed because it criticised their false beliefs and bogus religious practices, the reply was, "Who is more evil than the one who fabricates lies about Allah or denies His verses? Surely, the evil doers will not be successful" (17).

The human habit of turning to Allah in times of hardship is proof of "the inbuilt faith in Allah." This deep-rooted faith comes to the surface when we face hardships, we naturally turn to Allah but, as soon as the hardship is over, we return to the old ways. "He lets you travel by land and sea, when you are on board a ship, sailing joyfully along with a favourable wind, suddenly stormy winds blow, waves from every direction, they realise they are engulfed; now they pray to Allah, sincerely and faithfully, "If You save us from this, we will be forever grateful." However, no sooner does He rescue them then, without any right, they start to act disrespectfully (22 -23).

The temporary and fleeting nature of life is represented in the parable of the withered crops. "This worldly life is like the water

We send down from the sky, it soaks the soil and grows the plants, that are eaten by people and livestock. They grow until the land takes on beautiful colours looking attractive, and its owner thinks he's got it! then Our command comes in a moment, and We leave it looking like stubble, as though it never existed yesterday" (23-24).

What is the reality of idols? They are "their imagined gods," (30), helpless and powerless. "Say, 'Can any of your idols begin the Creation and then recreate it?'" (34). If they can't then why don't they turn to Allah?

When they accused the Messenger ﷺ of making up the revelation and writing the Quran himself, the Prophet ﷺ was told to ask them, "Why don't you bring a chapter like it and call whoever you can to help you besides Allah if you are truthful" (38). When they persist in their accusations, the answer is, "You are being deaf, dumb and blind" (42). The Quran warns that past generations of disbelievers were severely punished, so be aware that you could be next.

The guidance of the Quran is in its life-changing teachings. It provides elegant solutions to human misery. "People, teachings from your Lord have come to you, healing for the diseases of the heart, a guidance and a kindness for the believers" (57).

The short passage from 61 to 63 vividly describes the qualities of Allah's friends. These are people with unshakeable faith, righteous deeds, and mindful of their duties towards Allah. Beware, Allah's friends have no fear, nor do they grieve. They believe and are mindful of Allah, for them are glad tidings in this worldly life and in the hereafter. There is no change to Allah's rulings; that's a great victory.

The stories of the prophets Nuh عليه السلام, Musa عليه السلام and Yunus عليه السلام are given as examples of past nations who refused to listen to their prophets. Each of them perished, so "listen or else you'll be sorted." Even the most arrogant and stubborn disbeliever, like the Pharaoh, eventually submitted when drowning. However, his repentance was not accepted as it was too late. "Today We shall preserve your body, as a warning sign for whoever comes after you. Unfortunately, many people are unaware of Our signs" (92). The remains of Pharaoh's body still lie in Cairo in the National Museum, a testimony to the truth of Quranic prediction.

The people of Yunus are marked out as people who repented on-mass: "There wasn't a single community who believed and benefited from its faith, except the people of Yunus. When they believed, We took away humiliating punishment from them in this life and gave them the opportunity to enjoy till a set time" (98).

The Surat ends with a persuasive instruction: religion is a serious commitment to Allah. "I have been ordered to be a believer and told, 'Keep your face directed towards the true religion, in tune with your nature, and don't be an idolater'" (104-105).

Surat Hud [11] - The Prophet Hud ﷺ

The central theme of this late Makkan Surat is the history of human disobedience. The Messenger ﷺ and the Muslims are reassured by a narrative based on the experiences of seven prophets. It supports the line, "Prophet say, "I am certainly a warner for you and giver of good news from Him" (2).

Juz 12

وَمَا مِنْ دَآبَّةٍ

Surat Hud [11] continued

The response from the pagans was mockery and denial. They were warned of the dire consequences of their belligerent attitude and challenged to write ten Surats like it (13).

Prophet Nuh ﷺ preaches boldly. His people were prejudiced against the poor. They said to him "It is clear that you are human like us, and only the lowest of society follow you, and we don't see you have any special quality" (27). Eventually, the Divine retribution of the flood drowns them, but Nuh ﷺ and his followers are saved.

The story of Prophet Hud ﷺ follows in the same manner. His people rejected him by saying, "You haven't brought any proof" (53), so finally, they are destroyed. The people of Makkah were familiar with the ruins of the People of Thamud. Salih ﷺ was their Prophet. Their moral disease seems to be the caste system, discriminating against people from poor backgrounds. They were punished with a blast that killed them.

Prophet Ibrahim ﷺ is the next, he pleads on behalf of his nephew Lut ﷺ. Lut was sent to the infamous people of Sodom and Gomorrah, beleaguered by homosexuality. This is followed by the story of Prophet Shu'ayb ﷺ in Madyan, a prosperous community that refused to listen to him. Their problem seems to be double-dealing when doing business. He warned them: "My people let not your hostility to me lead you to suffer like the people of Nuh or the people of Hud or the people of Salih suffered, and the people of Lut are not far from you. So, seek forgiveness from your Lord and turn to Him in repentance; My Lord is kind and loving (90)."

The seventh story in this series is Musa ﷺ and the Pharaoh. The Pharaoh, like his predecessors, rejected the teachings of Musa ﷺ, and was drowned for his injustice and his oppression of the Israelites.

Lessons learnt from the Lives of the Prophets

The common thread that weaves through these seven stories is the rejection of the prophets, the punishment of the disbelievers, and the final victory of the righteous. The Quran in its unique way is reassuring the beloved Messenger ﷺ of a victory but is also advising him ﷺ to be patient, to perform the prayer and to accept this unfortunate human condition. In these stories, the reader is reminded that people rebel and deny because of the love of wealth, which makes them greedy and mindless. The antidote is to believe in the resurrection and to reform yourselves. To overcome prejudice against the poor, be thankful to Allah and accept the Prophet ﷺ.

Why does the Quran tell so many stories? "We tell you the stories of the messengers to make your heart strong, and what has come to you in this account is the truth, as well as a warning and a reminder for the believers." (120).

In conclusion, humanity is divided into two groups: the blessed heirs of Paradise, and the wretched inhabitants of Hellfire.

Surat Yusuf [12] - Joseph

A late Makkan Surat called "the most beautiful story." It tells the story of Prophet Yusuf ﷺ It employs a commanding lyrical narrative, with an intriguing drama woven around moral and spiritual values. Values that are deeply embedded in Quranic guidance: truthfulness, patience, modesty, justice, forgiveness, kindness and courage

They are presented in a variety of contexts in this story, to prove that in the end, goodness wins over tyranny and immorality.

Through its twenty-seven episodes, Surat Yusuf effectively plots the complexity of human life and sudden and unexpected changes in fortunes. One day living at home, the next languishing in a dark, dank well. One moment enjoying life in a palace, the next in a prison cell; one moment a prisoner, the next a Prince. Here are the first 11 episodes mentioned in Juz 12:

1. Young Yusuf Dreams that eleven stars, the sun and moon are prostrating to him. His father Yaqub cautions him 'don't tell your brothers unless they plot against you.'
2. Yusuf couldn't keep his dream secret so reveals the dream to his half-brothers. The brothers hatch a nasty plot. They are jealous so they plot to kill him.
3. Yusuf accompanies his brothers to a picnic, but they tie him up inside a disused well. A caravan passing by picks him up.
4. Yusuf is sold as a slave to the King of Egypt's Chamberlain.
5. Yusuf is incredibly handsome. The chamberlain's wife, Zulaikha is infatuated with him and tries to seduce him.
6. Yusuf prays to Allah for help and by the grace of Allah is saved from her advances.
7. The rumours of the encounter soon spread and give a bad name to Zulaikha.
8. Yusuf is thrown into prison where he begins to teach and preach to the prisoners.
9. Two inmates, the baker and the butler, have dreams and Yusuf interprets their dreams. His interpretation comes true. The butler goes back to the King's court and mentions Yusuf to the king.
10. The butler returns to Yusuf and asks him to interpret one of the King's dreams. Yusuf interprets it and also gives the King a solution to overcome the looming famine that will ruin his country.

11. The King is fascinated by this interpretation and asks Yusuf to appear before him, Yusuf demands that first his name must be cleared so that the Chamberlin knows he was innocent. Zulaikha admits her infatuation and her sin and Yusuf leaves the prison, an honourable man.

The story of Yusuf ﷺ provides a real-life illustration of a Quranic principle: "It may well be that you dislike a thing yet it is good for you, and it may well be that you love something, yet it is bad for you: and Allah knows, but you don't know" (2:216). The Surat teaches life on earth is an extraordinary gift, full of trials and tribulations, but with endless opportunities. The message is patience and perseverance give lasting joy. On the other hand, short-term, instant gratification can be damaging.

Juz 13

وَمَا أُبَرِّئُ

Surat Yusuf [12] continued

Once Yusuf's name was cleared, he agreed to accept the prestigious post of the treasurer of Egypt. "Put me in charge of the country's stores," Yusuf said (55), the famine which Yusuf had forecasted affected the whole region, so Yusuf's brothers from Canaan visited Egypt in search of grains. He recognized them but they didn't recognize him. He is generous to them and returns the goods they gave in exchange for the grains. But he demanded that they bring their half-brother with them.

Yaqub reluctantly allows Benjamin to go on the errand. As they leave for Egypt the second time Yaqub gives them advice on how to avoid the evil eye: "My sons, don't enter together through one gate, but enter from different gates. I can't shield you against anything from Allah, as ultimate authority belongs to Him alone. (67). When they meet Yusuf, he takes Benjamin aside and tells him who he is. An interesting turn of events results in Benjamin being allowed to stay with Yusuf (69- 77).

In the next episode, the brothers plead for Benjamin's freedom but in vain. They return home bearing the sad news. Yaqub is devastated "Such grief over Yusuf!" His eyes clouded over, turning white, such was his sadness; yet he controlled his emotions (84).

The great forgiveness
The brothers beg for mercy, Yusuf is touched by their miserable situation and declares his identity to them. "They said, "Yusuf, is that you?" "I am Yusuf," he said, "and this is my brother. Allah has

favoured us" (88-91). Finally, the family joins Yusuf in Egypt. His wonderful childhood dream is fulfilled: "As he invited his parents to sit on the throne, they fell before him in prostration" (100).

Surat Al-Ra'd [13] - The Thunder

This late Makkan Surat teaches the Greatness of Allah, evident in scripture and nature. Nature is an open book, where Allah's creativity can be seen, felt and experienced. The scripture teaches moral values that determine a person's faith and character. Spiritual ideals that fill life with meaning and answer the big questions: who are we? where do we come from? and where are we going?

The Quran insists people must use reason, and not wizardry. The Makkans employed many hostile tactics to oppose the Prophet ﷺ. They started a smear campaign, mocked, ridiculed and even made physical threats. Some Muslims wished that Allah would send a miracle so that their fellow citizens would see and believe. "Even if such a Quran was revealed that could move the mountains or destroy the Earth or make dead speak, they still wouldn't believe" (31). Allah doesn't want to persuade people with miraculous wizardry. Instead, the Quran offers reasons to believe, evidence from nature, physical phenomena, and human history. These appeals to human intellect and emotions can stir faith in Allah and motivate belief. The Quran wants people to decide for themselves, to accept Allah or reject faith. A moral choice has to be made since change only comes from within. "Allah doesn't change the condition of people until they change what's in themselves" (11).

The Awesome Creation and the Infinite Knowledge of Allah

The Surat opened with a list of amazing natural phenomena: the sky without pillars, the rising and setting of the sun and the moon, the vast mountains, running rivers, spectacular groves of palm trees, vast vineyards and fields of maize and wheat. The Quran disapproves of the disbelievers' stubbornness and rejection of the truth. All of this is the creation of a supreme, powerful Lord. What are their idols in comparison? The "intelligent people", believe the Messenger ﷺ.

To illustrate the benefits of the Quranic teachings a parable is told. Heavy rain floods the valleys and on the top froth floats. After the storm, when everything settles down, the froth vanishes but the valuable minerals and the life-giving water stays to nourish the land. The Quran will remain, and their idols perish.

Eight qualities of the believers. They fulfil their contract with Allah and develop good human relationships. The Messenger ﷺ is reassured and continues preaching confidently. Already signs of victory are appearing. "Don't they realise that We are advancing in their land and its boundaries are shrinking?" (41). This is a possible reference to the group from Madinah, who had embraced Islam and were now inviting the Prophet ﷺ to come to their city – a lead up to the Hijrah and the final departure of the Prophet ﷺ from Makkah. The Surat highlights the source of lasting happiness as the remembrance of Allah (28-29).

Surat Ibrahim [14] - The Prophet Ibrahim ﷺ

The Prophet ﷺ visited Taif to call the Banu Thaqif to Islam, only to be shockingly thrown out of the town and pelted with stones. The Surat begins and ends with a simple statement of the purpose of revelation: to affirm the Oneness of Allah and to bring people out of the darkness of idolatry into the light of Tawhid.

Why is true belief equated with gratitude, and so deserving of reward (7), while idolatry is associated with ingratitude (kufr)? Because everything we rely on for our existence comes from Allah. To pretend that it belongs to a carved idol is insulting to human dignity. Those who worship idols including the modern materialist are reminded (9-14), of the stories they knew about the disbelievers of Nuh, Ad and Thamud. A graphic account of Hell (15-17) should remind them that punishment in this world will not be the end of it.

The parable of ashes scattered by the wind (18-20), is told to give the ungrateful disbelievers pause for thought and to question the lasting value, if any, of the worldly wealth and power of which they're so proud.

The parable of two trees (24-27), one rooted firmly bearing fruit, and the other uprooted and rotting slowly is told next. "Allah likens a good word to a good tree, whose roots are fixed and whose branches reach to the sky; every season, it bears fruit by the Lord's permission. Allah gives people parables so they may reflect. Similarly, an evil word can be likened to a rotten tree, lying uprooted on the ground, rootless" (24-26).

The Surat ends with an account of the anguished prayer of Ibrahim (35- 41), seeking forgiveness for himself, his parents, and his family. The impact of these words would have been considerable on the pagan Arabs who prided themselves in their forefather Ibrahim ﷺ.

Surat Al-Hijr [15] - The Rock City

Juz 13 ends with Surat Al-Hijr, revealed in the final years of the Prophetic mission. The central theme discusses the Makkans' attitude towards the Prophet ﷺ.

Juz 14

رُبَمَا

Surat Al-Hijr [15] continued

They are not serious about spiritual matters, and love worldly life, "Leave them to eat and enjoy themselves, preoccupied with long hopes" (3). They were stubborn and unwilling to listen to reasonable arguments. So, they needed a good dose of moral and spiritual guidance, since their economic success had made them materialistic, selfish and greedy.

The Quran presents the fates of past communities who opposed their prophets. The story of Ibrahim ﷺ is told. He is given the good news of a son and informed that the people of Lut ﷺ would be punished. An example of Allah's kindness to his servant and the punishment of the disobedient.

The Divine promise to protect the Quran: "We revealed the Reminder, and We are its Protectors" (9), is a promise that we continue to witness today.

The story of human creation is repeated with emphasis on Satan vowing to mislead them, however, he is told he will not have any control over Allah's servants (26-50).

There are further illustrations of the disastrous fate of the people of the Madyan woodlands, and the cave dwellers of Thamud, after whom the Surat gets its name (Al-Hijr). The Makkans were familiar with these ancient communities since their ruins were on the trade route to Syria and Yemen.

Surat Al-Nahl [16] - The Bee

This Surat was revealed in the last months of 622 CE, before the Prophet's ﷺ migration to Madinah. The tension between Makkans and Muslims was high at that time. The Muslims were disheartened, while the disbelievers felt confident Islam was no longer gaining new followers. However, the Surat is optimistic and encourages Muslims to keep faith in the promise of a victory. It tells them, "Be patient, your patience is a gift from Allah. Don't be anxious about them nor distress yourself because of their plots" (127).

The Quran often mentions two kinds of books, the revealed Scripture that presents divine instructions, explanations and a set of beliefs. The other is nature, an open book comprising of the universe, the sun and stars, the moon, the flight of birds, the seas, pearls and rubies, ships ploughing through mighty waves, the rivers, mountains, cattle, riding animals, rain, plants, fruit, milk, honey and numerous crops.

This Surat is also called Al-Nia'mah, meaning, "the gift" because it lists a catalogue of gifts. Thankfulness is the only way to appreciate them. This is the very essence of Islam. Its opposite is un-thankfulness, the meaning of Kufr is that the Kafir fails to acknowledge Allah's gift.

The essence of the Divine Message is captured in this verse, it's recited in every sermon on Friday: "Allah commands justice, being good and generous to relatives, and He forbids indecency, all evil and cruelty" (90).

Allah created the entire universe for a purpose. How can we understand it? It begins by describing Allah's gifts, the domestic animals that were so important not only as food but as a means of transport. This is in the context of the fields of crops, vineyards, date and olive groves, and orchards. "If you were to count the gifts of Allah; you would not be able to count them; Allah is the Forgiver, the Kind" (18). Then we are reminded that the ungrateful were not let off but were punished. On the other hand, those who valued Allah's gifts will live in Paradise (30-33).

The Messenger of Allah ﷺ is there to guide you to it, so what are you waiting for? For further evidence investigate the history and see the fate of evildoers! Yet all things submit and obey Him. Allah's gifts are countless, but a baby must be the greatest. Apparently not so for the Idolater who feels ashamed when he gets the news of a baby girl. What a pity, the Quran laments. We are reminded of the patient nature of Allah that He does not rush to punish us no matter how wretched we become.

After this commentary, the Surat returns to the subject of gifts. Milk and honey are two amazing gifts. Milk is pure, nutritious food from the deep bowels of the cow and the honey from the stomach of the tiny bee. Two marvellous ingenious factories. The gift of Children and grandchildren. The disbelievers are chastised for neglecting them. The Quran expresses shock at such thanklessness.

Another list of Allah's gifts follows shelters, shields, and sets of clothes (79-84). We ought to appreciate these gifts because of the primordial pledge that our souls made. Those who break it are likened to "the woman who tears to pieces the cloth she spun" (90), what a waste of time and resources, utterly foolish.

The Quran teaches the equality of the sexes, "Whoever – whether male or female – does good deeds, while being a true believer, We shall bless them with a happy life, and give them reward equal to their beautiful deeds" (97).

Undoubtedly the Quran is the greatest gift! So, we are taught "When you start reading the Majestic Quran seek Allah's protection from the rejected Satan. He has no influence over believers who trust in their Lord" (98-99).

Faith is a valuable gift, what is its nature? We are told it lies deep in the heart. Love of the world can rob one of this gift. It develops by observing the lawful and avoiding the unlawful. To sum up this discussion of gifts, Allah praises Ibrahim, presented here as a model of the thankful person. "Ibrahim was an exemplary leader, obedient to Allah, pure in faith and didn't associate anything with Allah. He was thankful for His gifts, so Allah selected him and guided him on the straight path. Allah Says, We gave him the best in the world, and in the Hereafter, he will be among the righteous and We revealed to you, "Follow Ibrahim's religion, the pure in faith".

A final instruction to the Messenger ﷺ is to continue preaching politely and patiently.

Juz 15

سُبْحَانَ ٱلَّذِى

Surat Al-Isra' [17] - The Ascension

Juz 15 begins with this late Makkan Surat, it briefly mentions the Prophet's ﷺ miraculous Ascension. His amazing night journey from Makkah to Jerusalem, and then to the celestial heights, finishing in the Divine Presence. The journey is an announcement of the timeliness of the message of the Prophet ﷺ for the entire world and points to the coming glory of Islam. The Ascension took place on the 27th of Rajab, 17 months before the Hijrah in the year of sorrow. The purpose of this two-phased journey was "To show him Our signs".

This is followed by a passage retelling two historical events that devastated the Jewish community. In 586 BC, the Babylonians destroyed the Temple of Solomon and took the Israelites in captivity. The second event occurred in 70 CE, at the hands of the Roman emperor Titus. He persecuted and expelled the Jews from Jerusalem. Some think this passage hinted to the conquering of Jerusalem in the Khilafat of Omar but not a soul was killed.

The essence of the "Quran" is described as guidance to the straightest path. It reveals an explanation of the divine proofs and the disbeliever's inability to understand them. Life is a test of faith. The Majestic Quran is a recitation at dawn with special effects, providing healing and Divine Kindness. It is, an inimitable masterpiece, full of powerful arguments and the truth, revealed in clear bitesize chunks.

The essence of humanity is described as hasty. That's why we crave instant gratification and want immediate results. It also may explain why people love the now, the fleeting world, instead of the everlasting hereafter? To help humanity overcome this weakness the Surat presents a new, just and peaceful way of living. It outlines a new world order: here people are kind, patient and forgiving.

It is summarised in the Ten Commandments announced in this Surat: worship Allah; care for parents; give to the needy; give up the Seven Deadly Sins (wastefulness, miserliness, murder, adultery, dishonesty, blind imitation and arrogance) (23-41).

The Quran warns humanity that Satan will exert his maximum effort to misguide, so be on guard. Though, "Allah's true servants will be protected from his insinuations" (64-65).

The Messenger ﷺ was devout and spiritual so a special night vigil is recommended for him: "Wake up at night to offer voluntary prayer that is only for you. Soon your Lord will raise you to a glorious station of praise" (79).

The mystery of the human soul: "They ask you about the soul; say, "The soul is my Lord's command, and you have been given little knowledge about it" (83). The Surat opened with the miracle of the Prophet ﷺ and at the end mentions the nine miracles of Musa ﷺ, witnessed by the Pharaoh and the Israelites.

Surat Al-Kahf [18] - The Cave

Juz 15 continues with this Makkan Surat, which contrasts the nature of the spiritual and the material world, one permanent, the other temporary, one seen the other unseen. Humanity is tempted by the attractions of the material world but fails to realise the importance of spiritual life. These contrasts are illustrated by five stories. Each story is followed by a terse and helpful commentary, which instils the love, majesty and grandeur of Allah. The five stories are:

- The story of the sleepers in the cave is about young men of faith, serious believers, unwilling to compromise their faith. They confronted society's evil and abandoned their families to save their faith from an oppressive ruler. The story illustrates Allah's power of resurrection, bringing the dead to life.
- The story of the poor and the rich man reveals the nature of the greedy, self-centred, insensitive and hard-hearted rich man who is ready to pick a fight.
- The Story of Adam ﷺ and Satan provides a clue to understanding the cause of spiritual sickness.
- The story of Musa ﷺ and Khidr, the sage who explains serendipity, "making chance discoveries and understanding things which you weren't looking for". The paradox of outward actions and inner meanings. What appears to be harmful turns out to be beneficial, and a loss becomes a gain. The lesson is that we should accept Allah's will since His plan is mysterious and full of wisdom and our understanding only partial.
- The story of Zulqarnayn, the mighty ruler challenges the view that the world must be abandoned for spiritual growth. It shows that is not necessary to gain Paradise. What is needed is Allah-consciousness.

The underlying theme in these stories is major temptations that individuals face with regards to:

1. Faith: the young men feared the Emperor would forcefully convert them. Our faith is always being challenged by society. How well we face those challenges depends on the strength of our faith. The company of righteous people can help to develop a strong faith.
2. Wealth: we are tempted by wealth, we love it and when wealth opposes religious duties, we often prefer wealth. We are unable to sacrifice it and unable to spend it for the good of others. The solution is to avoid such deep attachment to the world.

3. Temptations of Satan: He tempted Adam and Eve. He tempts us all the time. How can we protect ourselves against these temptations?
4. Knowledge, competence and skills often lead to arrogant behaviour. Resistance against this is found in humility and in recognising one's weaknesses and frailties. The example of the humility of Musa ﷺ is an excellent model for us.
5. Power can corrupt and lead people to commit atrocities and injustices. Protection against corruptive power can be found in being sincere and genuine in one's desire to serve others.

In each story, the conflict between good and evil is clear. The five types of trials are like a thread binding these stories together. The Surat also features much travel, moving from place to place. The sleepers of the Cave climb a mountain, the rich man and poor man walk to an orchard. Musa ﷺ travels by foot and boat and the adventures of Zulqarnayn involve wandering from East to West with his army. All this is hinting that goodness is promised in movement and the search for Allah's gifts.

Juz 16

قَالَ أَلَمْ

Surat Al-Kahf [18] continued

The story of Musa and Khidr continues. Musa humbly requests to accompany Khidr, who reluctantly allows him but with the caution – don't question me. Three incidents occur. Khidr deliberately damages a fishing boat, kills a young boy and rebuilds the wall of a rundown house. Musa is annoyed with these actions and questions each one. But only at the end does Khidr gives an explanation: "The boat belonged to poor fishermen, I damaged it because the king was coming to forcefully seize all sea-worthy boats. The boy's parents were believers, but we feared he would distress them by being disobedient. The house belonged to orphans in the town and there was treasure buried beneath the wall. Since their father was a righteous man your Lord wanted them to reach maturity, so they could dig up their treasure. this was your Lord's kindness. What I did, it wasn't done by my will; you couldn't be patient about them" (79-82).

The fifth story is about the travels of Zulqarnayn, a king and a just ruler. Wherever he went he did something good. His effort to build a wall between a tribe that was harassed by the Gog Magog is the most interesting one.

Surat Maryam [19] - The mother of Prophet Isa ﷺ

Juz 16 continues with this early Makkan Surat that was revealed before the first wave of migration to Ethiopia, in the fifth year of the Prophet's ﷺ mission. It opens with the prayer of Zakariyya who wished for a successor. He was old, childless and worried about his heirs. The prayer is a reflection of his deep faith: "My prayer has never gone unanswered by My Lord" (4). Allah blessed him with Yahya "The soft-hearted, pure and pious" (13).

The story of the miraculous conception and the birth of Isa emphasizes the Power and Majesty of Allah, the one beyond the law of cause and effect. The first words Isa said are, "I am a servant of Allah; He has given me the Book and made me a prophet and made me blessed wherever I go" (31).

The Quran rejects the belief in the Trinity. It is completely unacceptable to Allah: "What a monstrous thing you have said! Even the skies would crack, the Earth would rip apart and the mountains crumble" (89-91). The Divine anger is a powerful condemnation of idolatry.

A highly charged conversation then follows between a nephew and an uncle: Ibrahim very gently tries to dissuade and win over Azar, his uncle from idolatry. The courtesy and logic he employs are persuasive enough to move even a heart of stone. However, idolatry makes one deaf, locks the mind and seals the heart. Ibrahim sets a wonderful example for preachers and obedient sons on how to differ politely.

There are four stories: Zakariyya and Yahya; Maryam and Isa; Ibrahim and Azar; Musa and Harun. They reflect a father and son, a mother and son, Uncle and nephew and two brotherly relationships. The relationships between prophets and their communities also reveal the great importance of human relationships. Faith bolsters these relationships.

A glowing tribute is paid to Prophets Musa ﷺ, Ismail ﷺ, Idris ﷺ, Yaqub ﷺ and Nuh ﷺ: "Allah favoured these wonderful men; the prophets from the children of Adam, and they came from those We carried with Nuh, and they were from the children of Ibrahim and Yaqub. We guided and selected them. When the verses of the

Kind Lord were recited to them, they fell in prostration tearfully" (51-58).

The Quran condemns those generations who were the children of prophets yet, "After them came generations who neglected the prayer and followed their lusts. Soon they will face the consequences of their evil" (59). Salah is a powerful expression of a person's relationship with Allah, the Lord. Neglecting it demonstrates a lack of commitment to the relationship. This is followed by four short passages about the disbelievers' denial of the resurrection, their plight in the hereafter, they regret doubting their prophets (64-87).

The Surat ends with good news for the believers: "The Kind Lord will put love for those who believe and do righteous deeds in people's hearts" (96). This could mean, The Kind Lord loves them dearly. The Surat continues "We made the Quran easy in your language so you can give good news to the pious and warn the opponents with it. How many generations have We destroyed before them? Do you find anyone of them alive or hear as much as their whisper? (97-98).

Surat Taha [20] - Ta Ha

An early Makkan Surat which clarifies how 'Allah guides humanity through His messengers.' It begins by featuring the story of Musa when he is returning from Madyan to Egypt. He is appointed as a messenger and given miracles. The Surat flips back to the time of his birth, recalling how as a baby he was rescued from Pharaoh's murderous plan. "I wrapped you up in My Divine Love so that you may grow up under My watchful gaze" (39). Musa heads straight for Pharaoh's court. A heated conversation follows, and the Pharaoh is angry, but Musa boldly invites him to Allah. Despite witnessing the two miracles the Pharaoh refuses to listen. He mistakenly believes Musa is a magician so challenges him to fight his magicians. A vivid description of the duel offers insights into the working of magic, and why magic failed. These expert magicians realised that Musa was not a magician, so they accepted his victory and his prophethood. The Pharaoh was enraged and had them martyred.

Even after this humiliating defeat and witnessing nine miracles, Pharaoh still refuses to accept Musa ﷺ. Finally, Musa ﷺ leads the Israelites out of Egypt. The Pharaoh chased them but was drowned. Once in the Sinai Peninsula, the Israelites enjoyed the freedom and were blessed with the heavenly gifts of quail and Manna. When Musa left them for a short while to visit Mount Sinai the Israelites under the influence of Samiri the Goldsmith, forged a golden calf to worship. On his return, Musa was angry with Harun for not stopping them. Musa cursed Samiri for his blasphemy.

As a commentary on the story of Musa, the Makkans are taught a lesson: the Quran is a reminder and warns of the dire consequences of rejecting the Prophet ﷺ. The Surat had opened by telling the beloved Prophet ﷺ not to be stressed by the sarcastic and scornful attitude of Makkans, and at the end, he's told be patient, and seek help through prayer.

Juz 17

اَقْتَرَبَ لِلْنَّاسِ

Surat Al-Anbiya' [21] - The Prophets

Juz 17 begins with Surat Al-Anbiya' and the central theme is the essence of the basic beliefs of Islam, monotheism, prophethood and the Hereafter. Minds distracted by the world forget the Hereafter yet it is drawing ever near. People are busy criticising the Prophet ﷺ who wants to save them. Allah warns, beware the past nations did the same and were destroyed.

The Makkans are criticised for being absorbed in the world. Life is not casual, like sport, it is a serious business. Just see how the entire world functions in such an orderly way, under the control of Allah. If there were gods besides Allah, then there would be disorder and chaos. A powerful proof of Tawhid.

The Divine judgement is presented through the instances of historical disobedience and how the deniers of the prophets were destroyed. The next section is about the creation of the universe, and how all living things were created from water. Evidence that Allah will recreate humanity. The beginning of the universe is briefly described: "the heavens and the Earth were joined at one time? We split them apart and made every living thing from water; won't they believe?" (30). Scientists talk about the Big Bang, could this refer to that? The disbelievers mocked the Messenger ﷺ when he shared this revelation with them, so they are cautioned.

A frequent theme in the Quran is Allah takes care of humanity. This is demonstrated by the constant repetition of His Beautiful

Names (the Kind, the Caring, the Loving, the Generous and the Responder). Allah is Al-Hadi, the Guide who sent the prophets.

The Quran presents a historical record of how Allah intervened in human history by sending the prophets and established a clear framework for human salvation. The Quran mentions only twenty-five prophets by name, yet there were more than 124,000 prophets according to one prophetic saying. In Islamic theology five of them command a special status. The Prophet Muhammad ﷺ, 'Isa, Ibrahim, Musa and Nuh. The prophets Ibrahim عليه السلام, Yusuf, Yunus, Hud and Nuh have full Surats dedicated to their life and mission. Many others, like David and Sulayman, are mentioned several times, symbolizing Allah's care. The struggles, sufferings and steadfastness of seventeen prophets are mentioned briefly. They pleaded to their Lord for help, but eventually, the Divine wrath destroyed the disbelievers.

The deepest heartfelt prayer of Prophet Yunus عليه السلام from inside the whale was, "There is no god except You; glory be to You, I was wrong. We saved him and rescued him from distress, and that is how We rescue the believers" (87). The conclusion is: "This is your community, a single united community. I am your Lord, so worship Me. Unfortunately, people tore up the unity of their religion; all will be returning to Us" (92-93).

The Surat ends with a delightful description of Paradise and the happiness of the believers. The crowning verse of the Surat is, "We sent you as Kindness for all people" (107). What a tribute for the blessed Messenger ﷺ! How wonderfully Allah boosted the morale of the beloved Muhammad ﷺ.

Surat Al-Hajj [22] - The Pilgrimage

Juz 17 continues with this late Makkan Surat (621 CE), focusing on the spiritual progress and the connection with Allah. The opening verses paint a terrifying image of Judgement Day, striking fear into the hearts of believers. Evidence from nature is presented to support its claim for resurrection. The seven stages of human life are highlighted presenting powerful evidence for the divine creative power. Secondly, "You see the dry lifeless Earth, and when We send down water it stirs and swells, producing colourful pairs of plants" (5). Presenting the convincing argument, that life was created by the Mighty Lord and it wasn't an accident of blind chance nor a product of a blind watchmaker. Instead, it is by intelligent design from the Powerful Creator.

The oft-repeated question, "Why are there so many religions?" is tackled. "For every community, We prescribed certain rites they devoutly follow, so do not argue about this with them; invite them to your Lord" (67). Allah will pass His judgement on them. The Quran teaches that diversity in religion is part of the Divine plan.

Hajj is the fifth pillar of Islam
The Makkans were familiar with several rites, since its establishment some 4,000 years earlier by their forefather, Ibrahim. However, the Quran clarifies the spiritual significance of these rites. Circling the Kaaba and slaughtering animals. They are not just mere rituals, but have a purpose and impact health, mindset and welfare. "Those who respect Allah's symbols show true piety of the hearts" (32). The Quran invites us to go beyond the outward observation of rituals to understanding their inner meaning.

For thirteen years the Muslims were persecuted in Makkah and this continued even after migration to Madinah. They were attacked several times. So, in the second year of Hijra permission was given to the Muslims to take up arms against their oppressors. "Permission to fight is given to those who were attacked and oppressed" (39). The consensus among Muslim scholars about war is that it is permissible in defence only – offensive invasions are not permitted.

The Surat then reassures the beloved Prophet ﷺ that soon he will achieve success, so he shouldn't be distressed by the hardships.

Examples of past prophets all justify the triumph of truth over falsehood. The Surat concludes by outlining what needs to be done to achieve salvation and how to avoid the terror of Judgement Day as graphically described in the opening of the Surat: "Believers, bow, prostrate and worship your Lord, live righteously so you may be successful. Always make strenuous efforts for the sake of Allah as you ought to make effort (77).

Juz 18

قَدْ أَفْلَحَ

Surat Al-Mu'minun [23] - The Believers

Juz 18 opens with Surat Al-Mu'minun, the central theme is faith in Allah and the resurrection. Both are interwoven into the purpose of life. This explains why a true believer is contemplative and socially active, unlike the "armchair" believer. The true believer is faithful, generous, responsible and humble. Avoids useless pursuits and is sexually pure. Honours contracts and yearns for closeness to the Divine. These traits reflect true faith, a generous spirit and firm conscience. A tranquil soul is ready to produce good works. This is the description of the truthful and self-sacrificing soul. The reward is Paradise.

Then follows a catalogue of proofs in the universe of Allah's creative power. The seven stages of fetal development in the mother's womb are vividly presented, like an ultrasound scan. This is followed by a history of disobedience and humanity's rejection of many prophets. The disbeliever's seven traits are that they believe Prophets are only human and there is no life after death. They show nothing but contempt for the prophets, rely on false hopes and even hate the truth. They are stubborn and follow their whims.

Their criticism of the prophets is rejected as baseless, arising from their arrogance and confusion. They doggedly follow their whims. The life stories of some prophets inform the blessed Messenger ﷺ that the Makkans are behaving like the ancient people. (23-80). It points to the unity of the universal message of the prophets.

The disbelievers frequently called for the punishment to come quickly, but such demands were rejected. Allah gives them time to reform. Those who continued asking for miracles were also refused and told to use their Allah-given faculties of hearing, seeing and feeling. Finally, they were cautioned against the severe punishment of Hell.

Three questions are asked: "Who owns the earth?"; "Who is the Lord of the Seven Heavens?"; and "In whose hands lies the control of all things?". Their response is "Allah", so they're asked why not accept the resurrection? The Surat concludes by highlighting the success that awaits believers and reiterates the purpose of life as a time of preparation for the Hereafter (109-118).

Surat Al-Nur [24] - The Light

Juz 18 continues with Surat Al-Nur, revealed in Madinah in 5 AH. The central theme is social manners. The aim is to lay down firm foundations for building relationships between men and women based on modesty and respect. The penalty for adultery and slander against innocent people is given. There is a severe penalty for adultery. The mixing of men and women is proscribed. Hijab is the principle of modesty and includes behaviour as well as the dress code for men and women. Personal privacy inside and outside the home is sacred. These rules aim to develop a pure and decent environment, free of sexual exploitation. If sexuality is not controlled, it can cause disorder in family life and chaos in the wider society. These rules are powerful preventative measures that restrict shameful behaviour. Ignoring them leads to the spread of all kinds of sexual exploitation, indecency, pornography and prostitution.

The story of the false accusation against Aisha – the Mother of the Believers – highlights the importance of these social regulations. The story concludes by declaring her innocence and recommends six social rules; don't spread rumours, punish those who spread indecency, forgive, ask permission to enter houses, hijab for women in public and support single people to get married.

The parable of 'light' (35), brings us to Allah's guidance. In this parable the niche is the human heart, the lamp the Quranic guidance, the glass is the human intellect and the olive oil, the emotions. The example shows every person has the potential to accept the truth. Indeed, there is an inherent desire to know the truth. Like petrol, a spark can set it aflame. So, whenever the Divine guidance (the light) is presented, a person is moved to accept it. As we witness marvellous phenomena in the physical world, such as rain, rainbows and earthquakes, we are filled with awe that leads to belief in Him and we yearn for guidance.

Then an example of the disbeliever is given. He thinks and behaves well, has morals and manners that are pleasing. He believes he would reap the full reward for his deeds. What he fails to realise is that in a state of disbelief his deeds are worthless and have no spiritual value. Like a lonely, thirsty traveller he sees a glimmer of water in the distance, so he runs towards it. There he finds nothing because it was just an illusion. There is another type of disbeliever who is engrossed in the world, drowned in lust and the pursuit of wealth and status. He's sunk in hedonistic pleasures, lives in the pitch darkness of self-indulgence. He can't receive the light. The example describes the four layers of darkness: the darkness of the night; the cover of the clouds; the depth of the sea and tides upon tides. However, the disbelievers are told, "Anyone Allah deprives of light, shall have no light" (40). This spiritual passage comes in the middle of a legal discussion, the point being made is that religious laws are only meaningful and effective if Allah is at the centre of them. This is followed by a passage that stresses the power of the Almighty, and why we need to observe His rules. Devout believers are promised; "He will indeed make them successors on land as he made those before you successors" (55).

Four more social manners are pronounced. Visiting others, concessions in Hijab for mature women, eating together and the company of the Messenger ﷺ. The Surat concludes with a stern warning, "Let those who oppose His orders be aware, lest they are afflicted by suffering or receive painful punishment" (61).

Surat Al-Furqan [25] - The Benchmark for Right and Wrong

Juz 18 continues with Surat Al-Furqan. It opens by declaring the power and might of the exalted Lord, the Controller of the universe. Then provides the arguments for the Oneness of God (Tawhid), the communication of His Message (Risala) and life after death (Akhira). These beliefs were most at odds with pagan beliefs.

In Makkah, the Messenger ﷺ was constantly criticised. The Makkans were puzzled as to why the Quran was revealed gradually, rather than all at once. They accused the Messenger ﷺ of lying and argued that he was merely telling stories of the ancient people. Similarly, they targeted his person, why would a messenger of Allah be a mere mortal?

Juz 19

وَقَالَ ٱلَّذِينَ

Surat Al-Furqan [25] continued

The disbelievers are warned of the dreadful consequences of rejecting faith: "Can you can be a guardian for someone who makes a god of his whims?" (43). Turning to the natural world it points out the amazing creative power of Allah: the shadow, the nightfall, the rain, seawater, blood and marriage relatives, the constellations, the sun and the moon: "These are signs for him who wishes to be reminded of the reality" (62). A two-pronged approach is adopted to answering the disbelievers' criticism. Firstly, an argumentative approach which warns the disbelievers by telling them stories of past communities. Secondly, the use of reason and science. They are told to observe the signs in nature because they point to their creator. So, won't you believe?

On Judgement Day people will regret making the wrong types of friends. What use is regretting now! The Quran laments, had they read, believed and followed Islam they wouldn't be regretting.

Past generations who denied Allah were wiped out. They made their whims, their gods and did not listen to their Prophets. Their attention is drawn to nature, take the shadow. "Don't you see how Your Lord makes it get longer and longer, if He wanted, He could have fixed its size. We made the sun a pointer to His existence, then we gradually shorten the shadow". (45-46). That life on earth, depends wholly on water is highlighted in the next passage. This is followed by a beautiful description of the constellations in the sky, the stars, the sun and the moon. And finally "He made the night and day to follow each other, a sign for anyone who wants to be reminded of Allah's power or wants to be thankful" (48-62).

The final passage catalogues the qualities of the pious. They are humble, peace-loving, prayerful, moderate, and repentant. They don't squander wealth, murder, worship idols, commit adultery, give false testimony, engage in useless activities nor follow blindly. The Surat concludes with the prayer of the pious: "Our Lord, give us happiness in our spouses and children and make us leaders of the pious people" (74). Effectively, recapping the opening statement that Allah is in control of the universe and His servant submits and prays for divine intervention.

Surat Al-Shu'ara' [26] - The Poets

Juz 19 continues with Surat Al-Shu'ara' where the beloved Messenger ﷺ was teaching Islam day and night, but only a handful of souls followed him in Makkah. The opposition was growing. But, he still continued praying his heartfelt prayers for the people, during long night vigils and continued crying to Allah for their guidance. He was ever hopeful that they would accept Islam.

The stories of seven prophets are retold, how they were rejected by their people. The history of human disobedience is repeated once more. Perhaps, this is a reflection of how humans are prone to self-deception. Since they love power and wealth, can be mindless and blindly follow fashion trends and thoughts. The Surat exposes both human weaknesses and strengths.

Next, there is the dramatic story: "Then Musa threw his stick down, so it swallowed their trickery at once" (46). There was no debate, the miracle was compelling, and the magicians intuitively knew Musa عليه السلام was a prophet. But the Pharaoh refused to believe. The story of each prophet is separated with the catchphrase: "In this is a lesson, though most of them will not believe, it is your Lord Who is the Almighty, the Caring".

Another compelling warning to reform, before meeting the same fate as the rebellious communities of the past, is given. The stories make the point that all the prophets had the same mission. This is perfectly summarised in "When their brother Nuh said to them, 'Will you not believe?'" (106-110).

Ibrahim expresses Allah's generosity: "But My Lord is Lord of the worlds, who created and guided me, the one who feeds and gives me to drink, and when I am ill heals me" (78-80). Prophet Nuh ﷺ highlights the discrimination of the wealthy against the poor, "Why should we believe in you since only the poorest people are following you?" (111).

The people of Thamud are criticised for their vanity: "You build a monument on every hilltop, what a useless activity! And you build castles expecting to live forever; when you attack others, you do so brutally" (128-130).

The story of Lut describes the sexual perversion of his people, "Among all nations, why do you lustfully approach men? And you leave your wives that your Lord has created for you. You are transgressors" (165-166). Prophet Shu'ayb ﷺ exposed the deceiving nature of his people.

The Makkan's accusation that the Prophet ﷺ is a poet is rejected: "The poets are followed only by the ignorant, don't you see them wandering aimlessly in valleys?" (224). The Prophet ﷺ is reassured that these are unreasonable accusations. How can the beauty, eloquence and life-changing message of the Quran be compared to the works of the poets?

Surat Al-Naml [27] - The Ant

Juz 19 continues with this Surat, which was revealed in the middle-Makkan period, the fifth or sixth year of the mission. It charts part of the history of human spirituality by reference to five prophets: Musa, Sulayman, Dawud, Salih, and Lut. The opening verses describe the nature of divine revelation as being guidance and good news. The proof of this proposition is the story of Musa and how he received divine revelation on Mount Sinai.

The story of Sulayman ﷺ is told. He is both a prophet and a king. A man of worldly wealth and spiritual devotion. This sets the scene for understanding divine mysteries. Allah gave him gifts, including the ability to communicate with various creatures – jinn, birds and even insects like the ant. The stories of King Sulayman and the Queen of Sheba are full of symbolism, and finely weave together the realities of worldly life and spiritual realities. In some ways, it represents the story of the human soul's spiritual awakening and eventual realisation of moral and spiritual truths. The story of the hoopoe, the speech of the ant, and the transportation of the mighty throne of Queen of Sheba thousand miles in the twinkling of an eye express great truths. There is a certain spiritual truth underlying each one of them, sometimes presented openly others allegorically. When the hoopoe told Sulayman about the Queen of Sheba, he dispatched a letter inviting her to become a believer and give up her idolatry. The queen decided to play it safe and sent precious gifts to him. Sulayman refused to accept her gifts. She wisely decided to meet him in person, travelled from Saba to Jerusalem. In the story of the hoopoe, the Quran teaches the lesson that a bird can sometimes have knowledge of things that even experts may lack, so don't be arrogant.

Next is the story of Prophet Salih ﷺ and Prophet Lut ﷺ who faced serious opposition from their people. It contrasts with the story of the Queen of Sheba, who eagerly accepted faith and realised the foolishness of idolatry. The severe opposition and the hostility faced by these two prophets is a commentary on the human condition. People are warned against thoughtless addiction to materialism and idolatry. Instead, become like the Queen of Sheba.

Juz 20

أَمَّنْ خَلَقَ

Surat Al-Naml [27] continued

A question is asked, who saves you when you are in hardship? Another section follows in which the question of the creator is raised, is there another God besides Allah? They accept Allah is the absolute creator with immense knowledge. So, why not believe? A mysterious creature is mentioned: "When the judgement against them comes to pass, We shall bring out a creature from the Earth that will speak to them; indeed people did not believe in our signs" (82). It is the prediction of the Quran and the books of hadith that hint when this creature comes it will trigger the beginning of the end of the world.

Surat Al-Qasas [28] - The Story

Juz 20 continues with Surat Al-Qasas. It was revealed before the Ascension of the Prophet ﷺ in the 10th year of his mission. It relates several stories from the life of Musa to show that history keeps repeating itself. A convincing consolation for the Messenger ﷺ and his followers. It opens by describing the Pharaoh oppressing the Israelites, and his policy of "divide and rule". This is a story of the survival of baby Musa at a time of Pharaoh's policy to kill all newborns. The Pharaoh, Ramses II ruled Egypt in the thirteenth century BC. Allah protected Musa and nurtured him in the opulent palace of the Pharaoh. The story highlights the weakness of a worldly king, who is unable to distinguish between friend and foe, yet claims to be an "Almighty god".

Next, Musa kills an Egyptian in self-defence of an Israelite. Musa is nearly arrested but manages to escape. He hurriedly leaves Egypt and travels to Madyan in the Arabian Desert. He is given asylum by an elderly man. Musa agrees to live and work for him in return for marriage to his daughter. Musa, who had been raised as a prince in a palace, now becomes a poor shepherd in the desert – a sharp contrast in lifestyle. The Divine Plan has its own way of unfolding reality. As a shepherd, Musa was being trained for the role of leadership. Looking after, a flock of sheep is not much different from caring for a complaining and undisciplined community.

After ten years, Musa ﷺ returns to Egypt. On the way, he passes Mount Sinai, where he is commissioned as a prophet to invite the Pharaoh to accept guidance. After relating his story in detail, the Quran reminds the Prophet ﷺ, "You weren't present on the western side of the mountain when we ordained Musa with the Commandments" (44). The Quran asks, isn't this proof the Prophet ﷺ receives revelation.

The Quran rejects the request of the Makkans for a written Quran and reminds them Musa had the Torah written on tablets, but still, people denied it. However, the Quran goes on to praise those people who believed in it from the Arabs, the Jews and the Christians: (53-54).

After a lengthy commentary that describes the fate of the idolaters in the Hereafter (54-75), the Surat returns to the story of Musa with an account of Qarun, the wealthiest Israelite in Egypt. It describes his pompous lifestyle, his miserly attitude and pride. The stories of Pharaoh and Qarun, expose the human craving for worldly power and wealth and contrast them with Musa's humble efforts. The cold-hearted way Pharaoh maintained a tight grip on his people and the miserliness of Qarun show human greed at its worst. He ascribed his wealth to his knowledge and expertise in business and prudence in worldly affairs. Similarly, the leaders of Makkah refused to believe, like them, they feared losing control of the Kaaba and the wealth it brought. Such reasoning continues today, as many of us fail to live by the Quran due to fear of worldly losses.

Surat Al-'Ankabut [29] - The Spider

Juz 20 continues with Surat Al-'Ankabut. This is the last Surat revealed in Makkah. Its confrontational character is tempered by rational and historical evidence warning the people of Makkah against their folly. The intense persecution made it dangerous to be followers of the beloved Messenger ﷺ. The Surat opens with a reminder to the believers that life is full of tests and success comes by passing them. The reward for jihad, hard work and tireless effort is victory. What lies between the two ends are details and processes for achieving success.

The central theme is the constant confrontation between belief and disbelief – truth and falsehood, symbolised by the antagonism between Ibrahim and Nimrod; the tussle between Musa and Pharaoh, and the struggle between Nuh and his people. So, the Prophet ﷺ is encouraged to face the hostility from the likes of Abu Jahl and Abu Lahab.

The metaphor of the spider's web is used to convey the weak nature of worldly power, in contrast to the enduring nature of Allah's religion. The Quran says, "An example of people who take supporters beside Allah is like a spider making a web. Indeed, the weakest of homes is a spider's web" (41). Sharp criticism of idolatry, love of the world and denial of the truth. But what is at stake is so precious, that the Quran employs such devices to awaken the dead conscience of idolaters and people drunk with the material world.

Juz 21

اُتْلُ مَاأُوْحِيَ

Surat Al-'Ankabut [29] continued

The Juz opens with two instructions; perform the prayer regularly and be polite. The prayer is a protector, "recite what is revealed to you from the Book and perform the prayer; indeed, the prayer protects from indecency and evil. Allah's remembrance is greatest! Allah knows what you are doing. Do not argue with the People of the Book; be polite" (45-46).

Surat Al-Rum [30] - The Romans

Juz 21 then, continues with Surat Al-Rum. This was revealed in the fifth year of the mission of the Prophet ﷺ, at a time when tensions between the Muslims and the Quraysh were problematic. The Surat opens with a remarkable prediction: "The Romans were defeated in a nearby country, but within a few years of their defeat they will be victorious.' (2-4). In 615 CE, the Persians defeated the Romans. Their defeat made the Quraysh happy. They saw it as an omen that the Muslims who were closer to the Christians would be defeated too. The idea that the Romans would recover from this terrible defeat was not credible to the Quraysh. However, the Quran predicted otherwise and indeed the Quranic prediction was fulfilled on the same day as the Battle of Badr (624 CE).

The central theme of the Surat is the creative power of Allah that reinforces the belief in the resurrection. It explains the underlying problem with the disbelievers' materialistic mindset, "They know the outward nature of this worldly life well but are ignorant of life Hereafter" (7).

Fitrah is the natural human state: "Stand firmly for the religion of Islam dedicated only to Allah. This is the natural human character; all humanity is created with it" (30). This is the human potential that flourishes when Islamic teachings are practised. It is the inborn, intuitive ability to discern between right and wrong, true and false, and sense God's existence and oneness (Asad). A positive, pure and near-perfect vision of humanity and a far cry from Thomas Hobbes image of beastly, brutal and selfish humanity.

We can't fail to see all around us wonderful and awesome signs that point to Allah's creative power. Some are brought to our attention: the creation of humanity from the elements, the love between husband and wife, differences in language and people's colour, the functions of night and day, the lightning and the winds. These natural phenomena point to their Creator, and the Quran urges readers to progress onto the next stage – recognise Allah as the Creator, worthy of worship.

The second prediction of this Surat is "Corruption has appeared on land and sea, an outcome of people's actions, so they may taste something of the fruits of their actions" (41). A possible reference to the environmental crisis we face today.

A third remarkable prediction is "On the Day of the Final Hour, the guilty will swear, they didn't stay on Earth but an hour; that's how they were deceived in worldly life. Those who were given knowledge and faith will say, "You were slow in accepting what Allah has revealed until the Day of Resurrection; this is the Day of Resurrection" (55-56). This foretells that Islam will continue until the end of time and the true believers will be on earth till the Last Day. Good news, that despite setbacks, the Ummah will flourish.

The Messenger ﷺ is given encouraging advice: "Therefore, be patient. Indeed, Allah's promise is true, so let not the disbelievers frighten you" (60). The Surat closes with a positive message just as it opened with a prediction.

Surat Luqman [31] - Luqman the Wise

Surat Luqman is next in Juz 21. Luqman was a legendary sage, a black Nubian and a wise man from Southern Egypt. By narrating his polite and instructive teachings, the Quran is promoting diversity of cultures, races and languages. The Surat opens with a vivid description of the 'devout Muslim': he benefits from the teachings of the Quran; stays away from useless activities that distract from the worship of Allah.

Sometimes the blessed Messenger ﷺ would teach the Quran sitting around the Kaaba, a Makkan storyteller, Nadhar ibn Harith, would also gather people around him to entertain them with Persian stories and dancers. The Quran condemned him.

People enjoy Allah's visible and invisible gifts so, "What have the idols created?" Luqman teaches his son the truthful beliefs about Allah, how to worship Him, how to behave justly with others, especially parents, and how to be humble. The final passage describes the natural world and several signs of Allah's creative power and contrasts it with human feebleness.

Surat Al-Sajdah [32] - The Prostration

Juz 21 continues with Surat Al-Sajda. At a time when debates raged about three key beliefs of Islam. The Surat opens with a confident assertion that refutes the disbeliever's objection that Muhammad ﷺ fabricated his message. The central theme is that Allah, the Supreme Ruler, the Absolute Governor and Commander, has full control. The disbelievers are warned of the punishment to be meted out, not only in the Hereafter but in this life. When they see Hellfire they will believe, but it will be too late then. On the other hand, the unimaginable delights awaiting the believers are highlighted to motivate people: "No one knows what blissful delights are hidden for them as a reward" (17).

Finally, the Prophet ﷺ is likened to Musa both recipients of Divine Revelation. The Surat reminds us of the constant confrontation between truth and falsehood and compares the glorious Quran with life-giving rain; the latter gives life to dry, parched land. Similarly, the Quran gives life to dead hearts and the dry minds of the disbelievers.

Surat Al-Ahzab [33] - The Confederates

Juz 21 finishes with Surat Al-Ahzab. This Surat was revealed in the fifth year of Hijrah (626 CE). After the indecisive Battle of Uhud, the Makkans wanted to defeat the Muslims, so in collaboration with the expelled Jews of Banu Nadhir, living in Khyber, they planned to attack Madinah. They gathered an army of 10,000 strong, consisting of many tribes, the confederates.

Juz 22

وَمَنْ يَقْنُتْ

Surat Al-Ahzab [33] continued

Background to the Battle of the Trench
When the Prophet ﷺ heard about the Makkan plan, he called a war council to discuss the impending danger. Salman, the Persian, suggested digging a trench between the long stretches of fortress-like houses on the outskirts of the city, whilst in the northwest, there were high rocks that were difficult to cross. So, a trench five meters wide, five meters deep, and seven kilometres long was dug in three weeks.

When the army of Confederates reached the outskirts of Madinah, they were baffled to see the trench. They camped outside the city near Uhud and laid siege. The only way to enter the city was if the Jews of Banu Qurayda were to attack from the inside. So, the Quraysh and the Jews of Banu Nadhir put together a strategy to win over Banu Qurayda and eventually a pact was agreed. But the plan went horribly wrong, and the confederates received no help from them. The siege was difficult to maintain, and the winter nights were long and bitterly cold. A violent sandstorm blew the tents. The camels and the horses of the Makkan forces ran wild. After three weeks, they fled. This Divine Intervention saved the Muslims.

This was a testing time for the Muslims. It required wise and brave leadership and committed followers. A large part of the Surat deals with the personal life and wonderful character of the Prophet ﷺ, and his relationships with the disciples and his family.

He is addressed on six occasions with the refrain "O Prophet!' to bolster his morale, reassuring him of his unique position in Allah's sight, and encouraging him to lead confidently. The following verse is also revealed:

In the Messenger of Allah, there is a beautiful example for you... We sent you as a witness, giver of good news and a Warner, one who invites to Allah by his permission and you are a light-giving lamp (21-46).

True followers practice self-control – a key to success in life. Special advice is offered to the disciples, who faced all kinds of tests; criticism from the hypocrites, the siege, lack of food and water and the continuous threat of attack. They had to control their anger, frustration and fear. The challenge was to resist Satan's whispers and refrain from losing self-control. The Surat highlights the qualities of the believers. They had unwavering faith in the mission of the Prophet ﷺ, they were grateful to Allah, truthful and honest.

The Surat ends by clarifying the purpose and meaning of human life, the proper use of "free will" and "moral responsibility". How we fulfil this responsibility will determine our eventual fate, Hell or Heaven.

Surat Al-Saba' [34] - The Kingdom of Saba

Juz 22 continues with Surat Al-Saba'. The central theme is the evidence for the resurrection. The scenes of Judgement Day are described vividly as though they are unfolding before the reader's eyes. Allah's Glory and Power are emphasised as humanity will stand in the Divine court.

Dawud and Sulayman were gifted by Allah. They were appreciative so, Allah rewarded them even more. By contrast, the people of Saba, who were blessed with a dam, dykes, fertile land and economic prosperity, were ungrateful. Thus inviting Divine retribution. The dam burst and the overwhelming flood destroyed everything in its wake. This devastated the agricultural land and that left them impoverished. Since the Makkans were familiar with this story the Quran doesn't give too much detail.

The outline of a conversation between disbelievers on Judgement Day reveals the horrific scene. At the end the Messenger ﷺ is proclaimed as a prophet for all humanity: "We sent you to all the people as the messenger of good news and a warner, but most people do not know this" (28). This is the declaration of the universality of Islam.

Surat Al-Fatir [35] - The Originator of The Universe

Juz 22 continues with Surat Al-Fatir. This is an early Makkan Surat. The central theme is Allah's countless gifts: the wonders of His creation in nature are a manifestation of his Kindness. "People remember Allah's gifts. Is there a Creator besides Allah who provides you from heaven and the Earth?" (3). Intelligent people can't fail to see the created world as the handiwork of Allah. For them, Allah is everywhere, "Of all his servants, only the knowledgeable fear Allah. Allah is the Almighty, the Forgiver" (28).

The Makkan people were stubborn in their denial of the Prophet ﷺ, so he is reassured, this is the wretched face of humanity: "If they deny you, don't worry; those before them also denied the messengers who came with clear signs, books and enlightening revelation" (25). He is told to be patient and resilient since Allah gives respite and time for people to think again and again. The stubborn disbelievers are given a warning whilst He is the Kindest, He is an Avenger who takes exact retribution. "Were Allah to punish people for the wrong they did; He wouldn't have left a single creature on the surface of the Earth" (45).

The three grades of believers are described in this verse: "Some wronged themselves, others were good and some by the grace of

Allah were foremost in good works," (32). To clarify, the three groups of believers are the "zalim" who make mistakes and are careless about their duties. The "muqtasid", or the moderates who fulfil religious obligations and avoid the forbidden but are slow with regards to voluntary activities. And thirdly, the "Al-sabiq", the committed who seek the pleasure of Allah, avoid worldly luxuries and never forget Allah. This invites us to reflect on our own condition and to assess ourselves. Which one are you?

Surat Ya Seen [36] - Ya Seen

Juz 22 continues with Surat Yasin, it's an early Makkan Surat. The Prophet ﷺ called it "The Heart of the Quran". Its central themes are proofs for the doctrines of Tawhid, Risalah and Akhirah. It opens by reassuring the Messenger ﷺ of the importance of his role in guiding humanity and laments the history of human disobedience. The chief reason identified for disbelief is arrogance reflected in human stubbornness. The story of three messengers, who were rejected by the people of their town, is told to warn the disbelievers. The brave supporter in the story, who stands up for the messengers, symbolises the small band of Muslims in Makkah, thereby reassuring them of Divine Help.

Juz 23

وَمَآ لِیَ

Surat Ya Seen [36] continued

The second section of the Surat describes Allah's amazing creative power and invites the reader to reflect on creation: a marvel of incredible complexity and beauty. Attention is drawn to the lifeless earth and how it comes to life after rain, concluding that this is how Allah will bring the dead to life.

The Trumpet will herald the day of Judgement when justice will be done. Evidence of one's good and bad deeds will not come, just from the records but, human limbs will speak out too. Indisputable evidence. A vivid account of the delights of Paradise shows how its residents will see Allah in His Glory and Majesty.

The Surat opened with two claims, the Messenger ﷺ is divinely appointed to guide humanity and the resurrection is real. Historical, rational and moral evidence is presented to prove this. The conceptual boundaries of the readers' mind are prompted to ponder the paradoxical: sparks of fire that come from rubbing together two fresh twigs. Indeed, "When He wants to do something all He says is 'Be,' and it is! Glory to Him Who controls everything, and you shall be returned to Him" (82-83).

Surat As-Saffat [37] - Arranged in Rows

Juz 23 continues with Surat as-Saffat. Its central theme is also proving the truthfulness of the Islamic doctrines: Tawhid, Risalah, and Akhirah. It opens with three attention-grabbing oaths that describe the perennial heavenly battles between the angels and Satan comparing them with the earthly battles between the Prophets and their communities. Six stories of the Prophets describe their courageous efforts to guide humanity. The dream of Ibrahim and his willingness to sacrifice points to the inner battle between the love of children versus the love of Allah.

Two scenes from Judgement Day are described: leaders and their followers at loggerheads, blaming each other for their dreadful fate. A pious person finds his friend in hell and reminds him of how he tried to misguide him, but failed in doing so. Zaqqum, the food of the people of Hell is a tree that resembles the desert cactus and has a poisonous sap with a foul smell which causes blisters and death. The Surat returns to the angels and how they are organized in Paradise.

Surat Saad [38] - The letter Saad

Juz 23 continues with Surat Saad, an early-Makkan Surat. It opens by describing the role of the Quran as a reminder, creating awareness and consciousness of a greater reality. This is developed by relating the stories of previous communities and the tireless efforts of the Prophets, starting with an account of the excellent qualities of Dawud and his son Sulayman. They were rulers and pious servants of Allah.

The heartbreaking story of the suffering of Prophet Ayyub ﷺ concludes the Surat. According to Tabari, Satan surmised that Ayyub would not remain faithful if he encountered difficulties. Allah allowed Satan to test him. So, disaster struck Ayyub: his house subsided, his livestock was killed, his family members died in an accident and he became ill with an infectious disease so that people abandoned him. Satan also attempted to shake Ayyub's faith through his wife, when she put forward the idea that he must sacrifice a baby goat for Satan if he wanted to recover. Ayyub refused to do this. In his despair and anguish, he prayed: "Satan has brought hardship and pain" (41). Ayyub is presented as a model of patience and endurance. This is what makes it a lesson, zikra, for those with understanding (43).

At the beginning of the Surat, the arrogance and hostility of the people of Makkah, to the Prophet ﷺ, results in the warning, "How many past generations We destroyed before them! They cried out; there was no time for escape" (3). The Surat also presents the other objections that the disbelievers have, to the message of Muhammad ﷺ. The stories of previous communities who rejected Prophets alternate with passages about the Makkans, facilitating a comparison between the two.

Surat Al-Zumar [39] - The Crowds

Juz 23 continues with Surat Al-Zumar. It reinforces belief in the Oneness of Allah and the dreadful consequences of denying Him. Professor Sells eloquently captures the mood of that early time, he says: What gives the early Makkan Suras their depth, psychological subtlety, texture and tone is the way the future is collapsed into the present; the way the day of reckoning is transferred from the fear and hope of a moment in the future to a sense of reckoning in the present moment. The centrality of the day of reckoning to the early revelations is based on a prophetic impulse to remind humanity of the moment of truth.

The graphic scenes of the Hereafter are presented in a variety of ways to emphasize the terror of Judgement Day. The severity of Divine punishment is stressed repeatedly, however, the pessimism of the sinners is dispelled, "My servants who have wronged themselves, do not be hopeless of Allah's kindness; Allah forgives all sins. He is the Forgiver, the Kind" (53).

The Surat opened by reference to Allah's Majesty and questions how such a generous Lord could be denied. We receive His gifts day and night: the air we breathe, the delightful foods we enjoy and the spouses that give us friendship and comfort. "If you are unthankful, then Allah has no need of you; He is not pleased with the thanklessness of his servants. But if you are thankful, He will be pleased with you" (7). Such fortunate people are blessed by Allah in an incredible way: "The one whose mind Allah has opened for Islam has received light from His Lord. But ruined are those with closed minds against the remembrance of Allah; they are grossly misguided (22)." The ability to see, feel and to speak the Truth is a great gift. The next passage compares the man of faith to the idol worshipper i.e. the modern materialist, "Can a servant devoted to many masters who are at odds with each other be the same as the one who is devoted solely to one master?" (29).

Juz 24

$$\text{فَمَنْ أَظْلَمُ}$$

Surat Az-Zumar [39] continued

Juz 24 continues with Surat Zumar. The unthankful person is selfish, follows whims and desires therefore, "The evil of what they did will distress them. The sinners will suffer the distress as a result of their deeds, and they won't escape" (51).

The final section of the Surat describes the way crowds of wicked people will be hurled into hell. The angels will ask, "Didn't messengers from among you come to recite your Lord's verses and warn you of the meeting on this Day?" (71). They will regretful. This is the purpose of presenting the Hereafter in the present: to jolt and awaken us. At the end, we read about the dignified entry of the believers into Paradise, with angels singing the praises of the Lord.

Surat Al-Mu'min [40] - The Believer

The next Surat is Surat Al-Mu'min, it opens with the claim, "This is a revelation from Allah the Almighty, the Knower" (2). The disbelievers denied this, so arguments from human history, experience and the natural world are presented. Their denial is based on false pride of knowledge and wealth, which deludes them. They mistakenly think material things will save them and that they have no need of the Almighty. Materialism is a strong attachment to worldly things to the extent that the people don't believe in anything other than the practical problems of their lives. "So, when Our Messengers came to them with clear signs, they smugly continued to enjoy their knowledge and eventually were engulfed by the punishment they mocked" (83).

The angels pray for the spiritually inclined: "Our Lord, everything is under the shade of Your Kindness and Knowledge, therefore forgive those who repent and follow your way and protect them from the punishment of Hell (7).

Scenes of Judgement Day describe Divine Justice in full swing. People's limbs testifying against them, people hurled into hellfire, angels scolding the people of hell and the graphic depictions of hellish torment – all combine to strike fear into the hearts of human beings.

Allah is Al-Mujeeb, the answerer, the responder; a lovely way of encouraging us to seek His Goodwill, Care and Friendliness. "Your Lord said, 'Call me, and I shall answer you'" (60). There are various stories, scenes and topics in the Surat with a common thread running through them all: Allah is the Almighty able to resurrect the dead.

Surat Ha Meem Sajdah [41] - Ha Meem Prostration

Juz 24 continues with Surat Ha Meem Sajdah, which was revealed in the middle Makkan period, after Hamza, the uncle of the Messenger ﷺ accepted Islam. Persecution against Muslims was at its worst. The acceptance of Islam by this prominent Quraysh leader strengthened the Muslims. The Quraysh held a meeting about the growing threat from Islam. Utbah ibn Rabiah, a leader, took the responsibility of 'striking a deal' with the Messenger ﷺ, so he went and said to him: My nephew…you have brought to your people something of grave concern whereby you have created a rift between the community… here is a proposal, see if you can accept it; if it is wealth that you seek then we will put together a fortune for you… if it is honour you seek we will make you our overlord…

and if it is that you cannot rid yourself of the spirit that appears to you, we will find the best physician until you are cured (Martin Lings).

The Prophet ﷺ said to him, "Father of Walid, now listen to me" and began reciting Surat Ha meem. Utbah was captivated as he listened attentively. When the Prophet ﷺ came to these words, "If they turn away say, 'I warned you of a thunderbolt like the thunderbolt of Ad and Thamud'" (13), Utbah put his finger on his mouth and requested him to stop reciting. On his return, Utbah told the Quraysh, "I've heard some words the like of which I've never heard before. It is not poetry, by God, neither is it sorcery nor a soothsaying…come not between this man and what he is about but let him be."

The Surat invites people to believe in Tawhid, Risalah and Akhirah. "This is a revelation from the Kind, the Caring; a book whose verses are clearly explained, an Arabic Quran for a people who have knowledge; it gives good news and warnings" (2-4). Why don't the disbelievers listen? Because they have locked minds and are intolerant. They should look at the wonderful signs of Allah's Majesty in nature. The power, wisdom, kindness, providence, organisation and management evident in the vast universe is a testimony that this is no drama or play of an imagined god, but the handiwork of the Almighty and the Knower.

The Quraysh are warned for their rudeness and rejection of the truth. Their arguments are refuted; Allah will raise dead bones to life, and a man can be Allah's messenger. They are warned: your behaviour is dangerous will have dreadful consequences. On that day even your ears, eyes and skin will bear witness against you.

The early Makkan Surats are conversational and speak directly to the listeners, each listener is asked to think, reflect and interrogate himself, for example, it poses a question like, "Say, "Consider this:" or "Haven't you seen" or "Haven't you heard". This teaching style isn't about facts and figures but teaches critical thinking to raise awareness of the Reality.

The Quraysh were prompted by the Jews to ask, "What is the need for a new revelation when the Quran already accepts the Psalms and the Gospels as divine revelations?" The reply was, "We gave Musa the Book, but disagreement arose about that too" (45). The Messenger ﷺ is reassured, he has a lofty, pure, beneficial, life-changing message, and if ignorant people fail to listen, then his response should be dignified, gentle and forgiving.

Juz 25

إِلَيْهِ يُرَدُّ

Surat Ha Meem Sajdah [41] continued

The Quraysh were prompted by the Jews to ask, "What is the need for a new revelation when the Quran already accepts the Psalms and the Gospels as divine revelations?" The reply was, "We gave Musa the Book, but disagreement arose about that too" (45). The Messenger ﷺ is reassured, he has a lofty, pure, beneficial, life-changing message, and if ignorant people fail to listen, then his response should be dignified, gentle and forgiving.

Surat Al-Shura [42] - The Consultation

The Makkans didn't just object to the belief in the Oneness of Allah but denied that a human could be a prophet. This objection is refuted, "The heavens are about to cleave" (5). So, absurd and insulting was their conviction. The central theme is the truthfulness of Prophethood. In describing the unique, distinctive and the otherness of Allah, "There is nothing like Him" (11).

A list of guidelines for inviting people to the way of Allah is given. Be patient, don't follow others' whims, believe firmly, be just, be tolerant, be responsible, don't argue, and finally, "Allah will gather you together and you'll return to Him" (15). "You will see the wrongdoers in a state of terror because of what they did, and its consequences will unfold before them. But the righteous believers will be in the gardens of Paradise" (22).

The message is one of making the right choice. Do you want the harvest of this life or the Hereafter? The mission of the Prophet ﷺ is to help us make the right choice: "Say, 'I don't ask you for any reward for this work, except, "love for the relatives. And whoever does a good deed We shall increase its positive impact for him."'" (23). The next few verses explain the wisdom behind differences in human capabilities. Without this difference in talents, status and aptitude, there would be no rank and file, no discipline and no organisation. People would be unwilling to cooperate with each other and consequently, human civilisation would not flourish.

The next section (36-43), gives nine tips for social harmony: forgive; obey Allah; pray; consult each other; give charity; be courageous; stand up for the rights of others. Then three things to avoid are mentioned, major sins, indecency and anger. The section finishes with "Whoever is patient and forgives, now these are things one ought to do"(43). A powerful appeal is made to humanity: "Come back to your Lord before the Day when there will be no turning back from Allah. You will find no place to escape that Day, nor will you be able to deny your sins" (47).

The Surat returns to the subject of prophethood, to dispel any doubts: not all humans can speak to Allah directly, so He sends His Prophets, with whom He communicates by revelation, from behind a screen, or through an angel (51).

Surat Al-Zukhruf [43] - The Golden Ornaments

Juz 25 continues with Surat Al-Zukhruf. It opens by demonstrating the unconditional loving nature of Allah, "Shall We turn away from you and deprive you of this Reminder because you are people who've gone beyond limits?" (5), no matter how heartless and unwilling people may be, Allah will continue to provide guidance.

The contradictory beliefs of the disbelievers are exposed. They believed in Allah as the Creator, but they worshipped idols. "If you ask them who created the heavens and the Earth, they will certainly say they were created by the Almighty, the Knower" (9). Another contradictory belief was the idea that the angels were Allah's daughters, yet they felt ashamed when they received daughters of their own.

They criticised the Prophet Muhammad ﷺ because he was poor and therefore unfit to lead. The Quran disproves them, 'Why was this Quran not sent down on a famous personality from one of the two towns?" (31). Allah shows His disregard for material wealth by saying, if it were not for the prospect of everyone becoming a disbeliever, He would have given the disbelievers so much wealth that the roofs, the staircases and the furnishing of their homes would be made of gold and silver (33-35).

The corrupting influence of wealth is illustrated by the example of the Pharaoh who declared: "My people, is not the country of Egypt and all these rivers flowing beneath my feet mine?" (51). The Pharaoh despised Musa simply because the latter did not have "golden bracelets". The Quran teaches that this is a mean and miserly attitude. Their objection to the Quran is rejected, "This Quran is a great honour for you and your people; you will be questioned about it" (44).

The Makkans were rude about the Prophet Isa عليه السلام also. They would say, "Are our gods better, or is he?" (57-58). The Quran goes on to praise the Prophet Isa عليه السلام and prophesies his second coming as the sign of the Final Hour.

The purpose of revelation is to caution people about the consequences of their actions in this life and to motivate them to accept the truth. What's the result? Paradise, where they will have "Food and drink in golden trays and cups shall be passed around. Everything that one desires, and the eyes delight in, will be there" (70-73). This is contrasted with the misery of Hell (74-78). The Surat opened by describing the loving nature of Allah, so it ends by advising the Prophet ﷺ to forgive his detractors.

Surat Al-Dukhaan [44] - The Smoke

The next Surat in Juz 25 is Al-Dukhaan. This Surat was revealed after famine struck Makkah. The dust blew and covered the city with a smoke cloud. The Makkans asked the Prophet ﷺ to pray for relief and promised to believe if they were saved. He ﷺ prayed and it rained, but they didn't keep their word, just like the people of Pharaoh, they broke their promise. The Quran tells the story as a warning. Some commentators believe the smoke cloud refers to a catastrophe that will occur near the Final Hour, possibly a nuclear explosion or the earth being struck by a comet.

A frightening picture of the people of Hell follows; fed from the tree of Zaqqum. Its fruit boils in the stomach tearing it apart. What a contrast to the delights that await the pious people of Paradise. The purpose of the Quran is to awaken God-consciousness in people. The Surat finishes with "So wait, they the disbelievers are also waiting" (59).

Surat Al-Jathiyah [45] - Kneeling

Juz 25 ends with Surat Al-Jathiyah. It discusses Tawhid, the oneness of Allah and unseats the idols. This seminal teaching of the Quran is the essence of Islam. The opening passage marvels at nature. The amazing signs in all of creation, point to a Creator. From the plant kingdom to animals, to the celestial bodies and the rain cycle. Attention is drawn to Divine creativity and the idolaters are invited to reflect on the helplessness of their idols. "This Quran is full of insights for humanity, guidance and compassion for a people with firm faith" (20).

The leaders of the Quraysh opposed the Messenger ﷺ because he was too radical and posed a threat to their status and wealth. They feared they would lose the income from the pilgrims if their existing belief system was replaced. They opposed him to preserve their hegemony and sought to defend their gods. They were not prepared to accept the Sovereignty of the God of Muhammed ﷺ. Too much was at stake. They are warned of the consequences of their rebellion: "When you will see all the communities kneeling down. Today, each community will be summoned to its Book of Deeds" (28). The Surat ends as it began, by emphasising the greatness of Allah.

Juz 26

حم

Surat Al-Ahqaf [46] - The Sand Dunes

Juz 26 starts with Surat Al-Ahqaf, it was revealed before the migration of the Prophet ﷺ to Madinah. A group of Jinn visited him on his return from Taif. The opening describes the helplessness of the idols and contrasts it with the creative power of Allah. Then explains how Allah communicated with humanity through His messengers, so the coming of Prophet Muhammad ﷺ was nothing odd. In fact, his coming was forecast by Musa علیه السلام in the Torah and Isa علیه السلام in the Gospels. The Quran comments on the suspicious mind of the disbelievers: "The disbelievers say to the believers, "If this religion was any good then you wouldn't have believed in it before us" (11).

The next section encourages the development of parent-child relationships. The mother bears the child, suckles and rears it until s/he becomes strong and mature. Just as we should be grateful to our parents and appreciative of what they have blessed us with, we should be thankful to Allah, our Lord and Creator.

The Surat warns the Makkans of the demise of the People of the Sand Dunes because they were rebellious. Finally, the story of a band of Jinn who visited the Prophet ﷺ is related as encouragement.

Surat Muhammad [47] - The beloved Messenger Muhammad ﷺ

Juz 26 continues with Surat Muhammad, which was revealed in Madinah, before the Battle of Badr. In the second year of Hijra, Muslims were given permission to take up arms against their oppressors. "Permission to fight is given to those who were attacked and oppressed" (22: 39). Muslim scholars believe war is permissible in defence only. Offensive invasions are not permitted. This marks the new era of hostility. The Surat opens by describing the continual conflict between truth and falsehood and urges the believers to be steadfast. Never surrender to oppressors and stand up against oppression. War is necessary to defend people's rights and freedoms, and to defeat evil. This is followed by images of the luxuries of Paradise; "There are rivers of water with never-changing taste and smell; rivers of milk whose taste never changes; rivers of wine that give pleasure to their drinkers; and rivers of pure honey; for them are all kinds of fruits" (15).

There were many new Muslims in Madinah, some were unsure and confused, even hostile. The following sections expose their plots and cynicism about the Prophet ﷺ. They were terrified of having to fight for the truth. Just as the Surat opened by highlighting the human tendency to war, it closes by encouraging the faithful to be ever-vigilant, willing and prepared to fight tyranny. This is a costly business, so they are urged to spend in the path of Allah. Selfishness and self-centeredness are sternly condemned.

Surat Al-Fath [48] - The Victory

Juz 26 continues with Surat al Fath. It was revealed in the sixth year of Hijra, after the Treaty of Hudaibiya. The Prophet ﷺ had a dream that he was performing the Umrah. The next day he informed his disciples. There was a lot of excitement, and preparations began for the sacred journey. Nearly 1400 devotees participated, with their sacrificial animals marked on their flanks, and garlands around their necks. When the Makkans heard of the coming of the Muslims, they were suspicious. They faced the dilemma of whether to violate the time-honoured Arabian custom of allowing anyone to enter Makkah or to stop them. The Muslims were stopped at Hudaibiya, eight miles outside the city. This was an unprecedented move in their history.

In the meantime, the Prophet ﷺ also dispatched his envoy, Usman ibn Affan, to seek the Quraysh's permission to perform the Umrah. Usman made it clear that the Muslims came only to perform their religious duty and were not armed nor prepared to fight. However, the Quraysh refused to listen and held him captive. During this tense period of negotiation, a rumour spread that he had been martyred. The Prophet ﷺ took a pledge of loyalty to die for the blood of Usman. A few days later, however, the rumour proved to be false, and Usman returned safely.

The Quraysh realised their mistake and agreed to a peace treaty. The two parties would not engage in any kind of warfare for the next ten years and the Muslims would be allowed to do Umrah the following year. This Surat was revealed during the return journey and pronounced a great victory.

Surat Al-Hujarat [49] - The Living Quarters

Juz 26 continues with Surat Al-Hujarat. This Medinan Surat was revealed in the ninth year of Hijra, following two events: a delegation of new Muslims from the Bedouin tribe of Bani Tamim visited the Prophet ﷺ and began shouting for him to come out of his living room. The Surat disapproved of their behaviour and laid out simple rules for respecting the leader. The second event concerned the misinformation given to the Prophet ﷺ by one of the Zakat collectors about the tribe of Bani Mustaliq. He informed the

Messenger ﷺ that the tribe was unwilling to pay the Zakat but this turned out to be untrue. This was condemned by the revelation.

This Surat offers moral guidance about living in a community and how to develop trust and overcome suspicions. In verse 13, the unity of humanity is stressed, uprooting any kind of discrimination based on colour, creed and caste. It points out our common origin: Adam and Eve. It teaches that honour and nobility are achieved through being Allah-conscious, mindful of Him and having a strong character. This is the foundation that creates equality and fairness in society. It is these values that lead to peace and trust among people.

The last passage of the Surat returns to the ill-mannered Bedouins and seeks to clarify the difference between true faith and ritual formalities of the religion, urging them to acknowledge Allah's favour. Faith is a special favour of Allah.

Surat Qaf [50] - The Arabic letter Qaf

The last Surat of Juz 26 is Surat Qaf. A Makkan Surat that argues for the truth of Resurrection and Divine Judgement. The sceptics are flabbergasted by the idea of life after death. The Quran responds to them by providing visible evidence from nature. The creation of the heavens and the Earth and the mountains and date groves from which they eat. Then evidence from human history: the ruins of previous rebellious nations. The Surat eloquently asks, "Has the first creation tired Us out? Not at all, but they are doubtful about the possibility of a new creation" (15).

The next section is: "We created the human being, and We know exactly what his desires are urging him to do; in fact, We are nearer to him than his jugular vein" (16). This verse highlights human whims, desires and lusts but warns that everything humans say and do is accurately recorded for, on Judgement Day, this will lead either to Paradise or Hell. Here, the Surat vividly paints contrasting scenes of Paradise and Hell. Towards its close, it reminds the reader of Allah's creative power and how easy it is for Him to create. Man is advised to celebrate the glory and praise of Allah. The Prophet ﷺ is prompted: continue to remind people but you can't force religion into people's hearts.

Surat Al-Dhariyat [51] - Gale force winds

Juz 26 ends with Surat Al-Dhariyat, a series of oaths about the wind. Wind is a fundamental element of life on Earth. It keeps the water cycle going. The implied question is: since wind is life-giving and is created by Allah, why don't you accept Allah's power to bring back the dead to life? Two more truths are highlighted: "And in the sky is your promised sustenance" (22).

Juz 27

قَالَ فَمَا خَطْبُكُم

Surat Al-Dhariyat [51] continued

Secondly, "We built the universe with our creative power, and We are ever-expanding it (47). Could this be a reference to the expanding universe?

The Makkans are reminded about their forefather Ibrahim who was blessed with a child in his old age, so He can gift a child to an infertile couple. This is another instance of the Quran challenging conceptual boundaries, which made belief in the Resurrection difficult for the Makkans. Then a reminder of the fate of those who denied and a warning to them that their fate could be the same if they persist in their denial.

Surat Al-Tur [52] - The Mountain

Juz 27 continues with Surat Al-Tur, a late Makkan Surat. It provides evidence from nature and human history for the truth of Islamic beliefs. It opens with five powerful oaths as witnesses of the message of the Prophet ﷺ and threatens the disbelievers of Makkah: "Your Lord's punishment will certainly come to pass" (7).

Verse 21 lends credibility to the proverb: 'you reap what you sow'; "each person is answerable for his deeds". However, a concession is made for righteous people: their faithful children will join them in Paradise, despite not being as righteous as their parents.

The next passage poses thirteen challenging questions: from challenging the mistaken notion about the Prophet ﷺ being a poet or a soothsayer, to who holds the treasures of Allah. The conclusion: the Makkans are a stubborn bunch, close-minded and intolerant. The Prophet ﷺ is urged to continue his mission despite their hostility.

Surat Al-Najm [53] - The Star

The next Surat of Juz 27 is Al-Najm. It was revealed in the middle Makkan period, when the Prophet ﷺ recited this Surat to the Quraysh near the Kaaba, they were mesmerised by its message and tempo and fell in prostration. The Quraysh's allegation that the Messenger ﷺ was misguided is rejected. It describes how the Angel Jibreel came to the Prophet ﷺ with Revelation. The disbelievers are told that they are irrational, lack historical evidence and are doubters. But the Quran provides knowledge from the Divine and its arguments are rational that appeal to common sense. The Surat distils the meaning of previous Scriptures in a pithy verse: "Each person will have what he has worked towards" (39), thus refuting the Quraysh's belief in the intercession of the idols. It ends with a warning: "The Judgement Day is near and draws ever nearer…Are you surprised about this? Laughing at it rather than crying?" (58-60).

Surat Al-Qamar [54] - The Moon

Juz 27 continues with Surat Al-Qamar. One night on the plains of Mina outside Makkah, the Prophet ﷺ was with a group of Quraysh, and they demanded a miracle, "split the moon into two parts, and we will believe". Abdullah ibn Masood reports that the Prophet ﷺ raised his hands and lo and behold, it split into two parts. The

Makkans were stunned, and quipped, "This is a powerful magic" (2).

The Makkans are warned about the dire consequences of their disbelief. The stories of four ancient people drive the point home, those who oppose God's Prophets always lose. Each story ends with the refrain, "How terrible were My punishment and warnings? We made the Quran easy to learn, so is there anyone who will pay attention?"

Surat Al-Rahman [55] - The Most Kind

The next Surat is Al-Rahman. This Makkan Surat enumerates sixty-two gifts and favours of Allah and asks a simple question, "So which favours of your Lord will you deny?" This phrase is repeated thirty-one times after mentioning two favours. People are challenged about how they deny the Majestic, Creative and Powerful Lord.

The first section of the Surat draws attention to the spiritual principles that underpin the existence of the universe. Just as the orbits of the moon and the sun are determined by Allah, so are the colours of flowers and the flavours of the fruits. The farthest stars and planets in space are firmly under His control. Everywhere in the universe, there is balance. Similarly, in human society, balance must take the form of just dealings with each other both in family relationships and in business dealings. In commercial transactions, everything must be written, recorded and weighed and measured accurately.

The second section presents a terrifying picture of Judgement Day. The harsh tenor of this passage reflects Divine Anger. A contrast with the luxuries, cool shades, delightful foods and flowing streams of Paradise.

Surat Al-Waqi'ah [56] - The Inevitable Event

Juz 27 continues with Surat Al-Waqi'ah. It warns the Quraysh of the dire consequences of denial. The cataclysmic events of the Final Hour and the coming to pass of Judgement Day are described. That day people will be divided into three groups. Firstly, those blessed with an exquisite Paradise, who strived for the nearness of Allah. Next the group of the right hand who will live in a delightful Paradise, a rank below and the third group, the people of the left hand, living in Hell.

The question of the beginning and end of life exposes the folly of those who deny Resurrection and urges the reader to examine closely some natural spectacles: who produces the semen? Who grows the seed under the soil? Who sends the rain down? Who made the fire? It teaches that human resurrection is no different from the birth of a baby created from a spermatozoon, or the nutritious cereals growing from a dead seed, or the flames of fire coming from wood or the rain coming from the clouds. These are all powered by Allah. He creates and destroys what He wills. The frequent reference to Resurrection reminds people of the purpose of their lives and prevents them from being deceived by the fleeting world. The Surat ends with a frightening scene of a person in death throes. Can anyone prevent his death? A powerful reminder of the helplessness of humanity at the time of death (95-96).

Surat Al-Hadid [57] - The Iron

The Juz ends with Surat Al-Hadid. It encourages the giving of charity to achieve the nearness of Allah. Charity demonstrates a person's faith in Allah and is an acknowledgment of His kindness. Charity is like giving a loan to Allah. In the Hereafter, it will be the light of the believers leading them to Paradise. The next section discusses the hypocrites, an uncharitable bunch, always in two minds, neither with the Muslims nor separate.

The Muslims are challenged, "Hasn't the time come for the believers, that their hearts humbly submit to Allah's remembrance and the revealed truth?" (16). A sense of urgency is imparted by this verse that encourages the giving of charity. Love of the world is a major hindrance to giving in charity, so the fleeting nature of worldly life is exposed briefly. So, don't be tempted by the world. Imagine a plant, started as a seed in the soil, it grows, dries, and withers away becoming dry stubble. Similarly, human life also has its blossoming period in a vibrant youth, an old age followed by a time of decline and finally death.

The theme of spiritual development is explored through predestination. Whatever happens in the world, or to people is all written down by Allah. Its purpose is to help people to persevere, endure difficulties and show patience at times of difficulty.

Juz 28

قَدْ سَمِعَ ٱللهُ

Surat Al-Mujadilah [58] - The Woman at odds

Juz 28 commences with Surat al-Mujadilah. Khawla bint Sa'laba was divorced by her husband and according to the Arabian custom of Zihar, when the husband tells his wife, "You are to me like the backside of my mother." This declaration could not be revoked, so the woman would be left in limbo, neither married nor divorced. So Khawla appealed to the Messenger ﷺ and this Surat was revealed to provide a way out for her from this difficult situation. This story illustrates that Allah is aware of our plight and our earnest pleas can prompt His speech. The Surat gives instructions about secret conversations. The rule is never plot to harm others. The hypocrites and the Jews plotted secretly whilst the Muslims were unaware of their plotting. The Quran teaches us the social manners of going into meetings and giving room to newcomers. The Surat ends by describing the dedication and loyalty of true

Surat Al-Hashr [59] - The Gathering of the Forces

Juz 28 continues with Surat Al-Hashr, it is a Madani Surat and was revealed after the Battle of Uhud, in the fourth year after Hijra, 627 CE. The central theme is the expulsion of the tribe of Banu Al-Nadir from their fortresses in the south of the city. When the Messenger ﷺ arrived in Madinah he made a treaty with the three Jewish tribes. The Jews welcomed this new arrangement, which guaranteed them peace. A Muslim woman selling her goods in the market was insulted by a Jewish goldsmith. A Muslim defended her and in the scuffle, killed the offender. The Jews killed him. The Messenger ﷺ asked them for the payment of blood money. Instead of honouring the treaty, Banu Al-Nadir conspired to kill the Messenger ﷺ, a clear violation of the treaty. But he left their castle safely. They were given ten days to leave and allowed to carry as much as they could. Their palm groves and homes were given to the emigrants. Eighteen beautiful names of Allah are mentioned at the end.

Surat Al-Mumtahinah [60] - The Woman Investigated

The third Surat in Juz 28 is Surat Al-Mumtahinah. The Prophet ﷺ would keep his expeditions secret, in order to prevent information leaking to the opponents. He planned action against the Quraysh leaders. Hatib ibn Balata, a companion gave a letter to a woman travelling to Makkah, warning the Quraysh. Balata's strategy was to appease the Quraysh and save his family, who were under their control. His plan was discovered, and the letter confiscated. He was reprimanded but no action was taken against him since he had fought in the Battle of Badr. The lessons we learn are:
- Don't base your judgements on guesswork
- Allah and His Messenger ﷺ have a forgiving nature
- Always be loyal to your community

Surat Al-Saff [61] - The Rows

Juz 28 continues with Surat Al-Saff. This Madani Surat motivates the believers to be brave and practice what they preach. To fight in the path of Allah when called to do so and not to shy away from the momentous responsibility of defending the community. The Surat criticises those who broke their pledge. By giving the example of Musa and Isa, the Surat challenges the Jews and the Christians to examine their Books. Their prophets had already predicted the coming of Muhammad ﷺ as the final Messenger. In the Gospel of John 14:15, Jesus foretold, "If you love me keep my commands, and I will ask the Father to give you another advocate to help you and be with you forever." Who was this advocate? Our beloved Prophet Muhammad ﷺ. Salvation is achieved through faith and Jihad, we are told. This requires a firm belief in Allah and His Messenger ﷺ, along with practical and persistent efforts to obey the law. Those who do so are honoured with the title, "the helpers of Allah."

Surat Al-Jumu'ah [62] - The Day of Congregation

Surat Al-Jumu'ah is a Madani Surat and mentions four important roles of the Prophet ﷺ: teaching; recitation of the verses of the Quran; purification and development of the character of his followers; and clarifying the Book with wisdom. The Surat highlights the importance of the Friday prayer, stressing the significance of this important weekly lesson, the sermon. Worshippers are encouraged to rush for the Friday sermon as it is an important socio-political gathering where the leader of the community addresses the congregation. The true believer will give precedence to the worship of Allah, over all worldly things.

Surat Al-Munafiqun [63] - The Hypocrites

Juz 28 continues with Surat Al-Munafiqun. This Surat is a commentary on an incident that took place after the campaign of Banu Mustaliq. A fight broke out between two men. One of them called out, 'Ansar! Come to my help!' The other one called out, 'Emigrants! Come to my help!' Both sides responded and swords were drawn. The Prophet ﷺ rushed to the scene to caution them and succeeded in calming them down. However, the hypocrites were jealous of this Muslim unity and began to plot and scheme.

Abdullah ibn Ubayy, the leader of the hypocrites stated, "When we get back to Madinah, the strong will expel the weak". When he approached Madinah, his son stood tall in front of him and stopped him from entering. But the Prophet ﷺ said, "Let him enter". Hypocrisy is vehemently condemned in the Quran because it smacks of an unprincipled attitude and disloyalty. The antidote to hypocrisy: give charity.

Surat Al-Thaghabun [64] - The Gain and Loss

Surat Al-Thaghabun deals with life Hereafter. It warns that wealth, spouses and children will be a temptation that could lead to breaking Divine laws. "Whoever can save themselves from greed, then those are the successful ones" (16). However, on Judgement day all will feel cheated, even the believers will feel loss because they will realise they could have worked harder for the Hereafter. The disbelievers will be absolutely devastated as they realise the world has cheated them.

Surat Al-Talaq [65] - The Divorce

Surat Al-Talaq is a Medinan Surat, which deals with divorce. It outlines the correct method to be followed, the prescribed waiting periods, maintenance and custody of the children including the breastfeeding of any child. These are like an appendix to Surat Al-Baqarah's passage on family law (222-242). The blessed Messenger ﷺ described divorce as, "The most hateful of permissible things" (Abu Dawud). Ali, the fourth caliph, said, "The Divine Throne trembles when a couple divorce." Islam allows divorce only when life as a husband and wife becomes so unbearable that it is damaging to the quality of family life. People going through divorce are reminded, "Be mindful of Allah." He shall provide them with a means out of this dreadful situation, and He will provide for them sustenance.

Surat Al-Tahreem [66] - The Prohibition

The last Surat of Juz 28 is Al-Tahreem. It tells the story of Zainab, the wife of the Prophet ﷺ. One day he spent extra time with her which upset Aisha, who complained his breath smelled of Maghafir, a wild tree on which bees feed. The Prophet ﷺ told her he had eaten honey and promised to refrain from doing so, in the future. The solution to sinning is "Taubatan Nasuhan" (8), sincere and genuine repentance. This means regretting the sin, feeling ashamed of it, resolving not to repeat it and then asking for Allah's forgiveness. Whatever the circumstances, five general principles are taught:

1. Not to make unlawful that which Allah has made lawful
2. How to amend and atone for vows
3. Not to betray trusts and give away secrets
4. The whole family should work together to save themselves from the Hellfire
5. Seek repentance for sins done intentionally or unintentionally

Juz 29

تَبَارَكَ ٱلَّذِى

Surat Al-Mulk [67] - The Control

Juz 29 starts with Surat Al-Mulk. The central theme of this Surat is the purpose of life which is an opportunity to earn Allah's pleasure and love by doing good works. The Surat points to the common failure to understand this simple fact. Those who deny will regret: "If only we had listened or understood the message, we would not be among the companions of the Blazing Hell" (10). The splendour of nature affirms the existence of spiritual reality beyond the material world. There follows a stern warning against failing to see beyond the material world, "Which forces beside the Most Kind can possibly help you? The disbelievers are only deceived" (20).

Surat Al-Qalam [68] - The Pen

This early-Makkan Surat warns the people of Makkah: if you refuse to believe in the Messenger ﷺ, then be prepared to face severe consequences like previous disobedient nations did. It opens by acknowledging the beautiful character of the Prophet Muhammad ﷺ: kind, generous, patient, forgiving and thankful. This is contrasted with the vices of Al-Walid ibn Al-Mughira a ruthless opponent of the Messenger ﷺ. And the story of the young owners of the orchard highlights the appalling nature of miserliness.

Surat Al-Haqqah [69] - The Reality

The core teaching of the Majestic Quran is faith in the Hereafter. The reality of worldly life is a mere shadow in comparison. The physical world is the apparent but the underlying reality is the Hereafter. The Quran, in its inimitable style, presents the Hereafter as "here and now". The Surat challenges our materialistic tendencies and reminds the reader to remember the horrors of Judgment Day. The examples of previous disobedient communities are a warning to the neglectful.

Surat Al-Ma'arij [70] - The Stairways to Heavens

It was revealed in the middle Makkan period. It criticises the sceptics who wanted the punishment to come sooner rather than later. Once the Messenger ﷺ warned a storyteller, Nadhr ibn Harith, of the punishment of Hell. He mockingly retorted, "Why don't you bring a sandstorm that will destroy us?" The Surat was revealed in response to this tactless demand. It reminds the questioner of the Majesty of Allah and the stairways leading to the heavens that can take people to their spiritual heights. This section vividly captures the terrifying moments of the end of time. The sky will turn red, the mountains will hang like fluffed tufts of wool and everyone will be full of fear and anxiety. The Surat ends by reminding us of the good character of the dutiful worshipper: caring and generous and in full control of his sexual appetite.

Surat Nuh [71] - Noah

This Makkan Surat sketches the life and works of this great prophet of Allah and his struggle against the unbelievers. The story comes as a reassurance for the Prophet ﷺ and the early Muslims. They would be saved and their enemies destroyed. For nine and half centuries, the Prophet Nuh ؑ preached tirelessly. He presented convincing evidence from the natural world around him and from history but, his words fell on deaf ears. The people were stubborn and couldn't see beyond the physical realm. The Surat presents a heartrending prayer, his moving sermon and finally his prayer of desperation in its final section.

Surat Al-Jinn [72] - The Jinn

According to Ibn 'Abbas, a group of jinn visited the Prophet ﷺ after he returned from Taif. The central theme is challenging the stubbornness and disbelief of the Quraysh. The jinn believed in the Messenger ﷺ whereas the Quraysh, to their shame rejected him. The jinn speak about believing the Messenger ﷺ and the Revelation, whilst the materialistic disbelievers think the Quran is mere poetry, or the words of a soothsayer or worse, a madman. It also reassured the Messenger ﷺ of the truthfulness of his message, building his confidence and self-esteem. The jinn are an invisible and intelligent creation of Allah, made from smokeless fire, a high-energy form. Like humans, they can be either believers or disbelievers. The Surat outlines some of their characteristics and some similarities and differences to human beings. It reveals their amazement and surprise at the inability of Makkans to believe in the Majestic Quran.

Surat Al-Muzammil [73] - The Wrapped Up

This is an early Makkan Surat, possibly the second after Surat 'Alaq. The first part of the Surat highlights the worries of the Prophet ﷺ about his mission. It describes the devotion of the Messenger ﷺ, his longing for Allah and his recitation of the Quran. The final long verse was revealed in Madinah and it gives flexibility to the Prophet ﷺ and the companions in relation to the length of their night vigils. The blessed Messenger ﷺ is presented as the beautiful example of a worshipper, who stands all night in worship, whilst others sleep.

Surat Al-Muddaththir [74] - The Cloaked One

The Angel Jibreel stopped coming to the Prophet ﷺ after the first revelation of Surat 'Alaq. This break may have lasted for a year or so and this was the first revelation after the break. The Prophet ﷺ is reminded of his important status and role in transforming humanity. The opening verses clearly instruct him to be energetic and forthright in preaching the message, without fear of anyone. He is being prepared for the hostility he will soon face. His opponent Walid ibn Al-Mughira is criticised. The Quran also presents this principle: "Every person is endangered by the evil it has done, except the companions of the right hand" (38). So, every person is a hostage only, of his own wrongdoing. An empowering verse.

Surat Al-Qiyamah [75] - The Day of Judgement

An early Makkan Surat with the central theme of the Day of Judgement. It describes the scenes of that Day: disintegrated human bones will be brought to life, a lunar eclipse will occur, people will be overwhelmed and confused. It will dawn upon them that they are standing in front of the Mighty Lord and justice will be done. They will see their whole life presented before them and still make excuses for their wretched behaviour. Abu Jahl once brought a decaying bone to the Prophet ﷺ and asked, "Can this be brought back to life?" The Surat answers him: "You love the fleeting world dearly" (20). He is warned about his death throes when he will die, and no one will be able to cure him.

Surat Ad-Dahr [76] - The Time

This is a Madani Surat, which asserts that humanity is blessed with the ability to distinguish between right and wrong and is therefore accountable. A terse reminder of the purpose of human life. Followed by a precise description of the good people. They fulfil their vows, fear Judgement Day, are generous and selfless and take care of the poor and needy. For these wonderful deeds, they will have the delights of Paradise. A reward for their patience and hard work.

Surat Al Mursalat [77] - The Winds

Five oaths describe the incredible power of the wind: from the calm morning breeze to the gusty winds that move the clouds, to gale-force winds that create storms on land and sea, and hurricanes and cyclones. The catchphrase, "That will be a Day of big loss for the deniers!" is repeated ten times. A counsel to the stubborn people: open your eyes, overcome your ignorance and egotism. And a stark warning to the disbelievers, of the consequences of their disbelief. A powerful rhetorical device for conveying a difficult message. Humans are reminded of their humble beginnings, from a sperm and an egg. The One who produced you from that embarrassing fluid is very capable of resurrecting you from the dead.

Juz 30

عَمَّ

Surat Al-Naba' [78] - The News

This Surat is critical of the Arab pagans who believed in one God yet worshipped idols and denied life after death. They failed to see the importance of this belief in ensuring a just and purposeful life on Earth. They couldn't comprehend how the dead would be brought back to life. So, they are reminded of Allah's creative power: vast landmass and oceans, lofty mountains, pairs of living things, the mysteries of sleep and nightfall and so on. The Day of Judgement will be the Day of Distinction. The Day when justice will be done and people will be rewarded according to how they lived. The final section beautifully captures the delights and pleasures of Paradise.

Surat Al-Nazi'at [79] - The Snatchers

This Surat is about the Resurrection. The story of Pharaoh explains why people don't believe. They are proud, selfish and love the world too much. The Surat opens with five oaths: war horses, winds, stars, the souls of the righteous, and the angels. The evidence leads to the conclusion, "You will certainly be resurrected."

Surat 'Abasa [80] - Frowning

One day, the Messenger ﷺ was preaching to the Makkan leaders hopeful they would accept his message. Abdullah ibn Umm-al

Makhtum, a blind Muslim, came unexpectedly and interrupted, "Messenger! Teach me what Allah has taught you." The Messenger ﷺ frowned at the blind man and turned away. The Surat commented on this incident, and thereafter the Messenger ﷺ used to say, "You are the man for whom my Lord censured me." The Quraysh were mistaken if they thought that Islam needed them. Instead, Islam appreciates sincere believers, like the blind man. The Surat also teaches respect and equality for people with disabilities. The next section highlights Allah's blessings: life, food, and fertile land.

Surat Al-Takwir [81] - The Shrouding

This Surat is about the truthfulness of the Majestic Quran and the validity of its teachings. It begins with the cataclysmic events prior to the Day of Resurrection. It validates the truthfulness of the Messenger ﷺ and the source of his message and describes the power, credibility and reliability of the Angel Jibreel. Finally, it challenges the reader, "So, where are you going?" (26).

Surat Al-Infitar [82] - The Cleaving

This Surat reveals the self-deception that turns a person away from Allah. After taking the oaths of the events leading to Judgement Day, it asks: "Humans, what has deceived and misled you from your generous Lord?" (6). The qualities of the Lord Who created everything are evoked to prick the conscience: you are monitored by the Angels who record your every move and on Judgement Day they will give a full account.

Surat Al-Mutaffifeen [83] - The Cheats

This Surat condemns cheating traders and dishonest shopkeepers. They are singled out since they have more opportunities to cheat and exploit the weak. Such injustices are committed by those who deny Judgment Day and feel they can do so without consequences. "Don't they believe they will be resurrected on a Grand Day?" (4). This group is contrasted with people of faith and honesty, who will enjoy the delights of Paradise.

Surat Al-Inshiqaq [84] - The Splitting Open

This Surat shows the connection between actions and outcomes, a fact discernable in the world. An indirect disapproval of the Makkans, who refused to obey their Lord despite having intelligence. Working hard for one's livelihood is a universal human value. But to limit life to this only is folly and so the workaholic is challenged. He is advised not to forget the Hereafter and the meeting with his Sustainer. However, those who work hard for their Hereafter are guaranteed progress, "You will develop stage by stage" (19).

Surat Al-Buruj [85] - The Constellations

This Surat marks the beginning of the second phase of the mission of the Prophet ﷺ, around the third year. It tells the story of the "diggers of the trench", when the Yemeni King burnt the Christians of Najran in a trench. This story gave reassurance to the believers and warned the Quraysh, the persecutors.

Surat Al-Tariq [86] - The Night Visitor

This Surat is about the truthfulness of Judgement Day. After taking the oath of the shining stars, people are reminded, "There is a keeper over you" (4). Those who denied the Judgement Day are invited to reflect about their humble beginnings. Where do you come from? And "Where are we going?"

Surat Al-'Ala [87] - The Highest

This Surat explains how the Majestic Quran and the Messenger ﷺ are reminders. The reference to the early Scriptures of Musa and Ibrahim verify the Quran as a continuation of the same mission. What blinds humanity to this reality? The love of worldly life. These verses express contempt for the love of the material world as it distracts people from their Lord.

Surat Al-Ghashiyah [88] - The Awe-inspiring Event

This Surat supports the three doctrines of Islam. The Day of Judgement is introduced in an unusual manner, "Has the news of the Overwhelming Event reached you?" Followed by a harrowing account of what will happen to the disbeliever who worked hard in his life but ignored Allah and forgot the Hereafter. In contrast, the believer worked to please his Lord. Humanity is invited to enjoy the delights of Paradise. Its elegant surroundings, its comfort and luxury. The price tag; faith.

Surat Al-Fajr [89] - The Dawn

This Surat opens with oaths that remind us about the binary nature of creation and the oneness of Allah. The Surat points out how humans are unthankful to their Lord. At the slight loss of wealth or pain, they grumble and become impatient. They are sternly warned and told to renounce their bad habits.

Surat Al-Balad [90] - The City

This Surat employs the metaphor of the steep mountainous track to describe the nature of Islam: a struggle, a jihad. Here Divine Dislike is expressed for people who are deceived by their strength and influence. Like the Makkan wrestler who thought no one had power over him, not even the angel of death. The Quran warns against such delusion.

Surat Al-Shams [91] - The Sun

This Surat opens with ten oaths including the sun, the sky, the earth and the human soul. The verse "Then He inspired it to follow either it's vice or virtue" (8), refers to the human soul. The Surat tells us that the human conscience can distinguish between right and wrong, between good and evil. Furthermore, the one who develops the moral values, spiritual beliefs and social norms will flourish and the one who disregards them will inevitably fail. The tribe of Thamud is presented as an example of those who failed.

Surat Al-Layl [92] - The Night

This Surat explains the diversity in human endeavour and enterprise. However, the primary choice of confronting people is between good or evil and practising moral values. Good people are generous, mindful and appreciate the good. Consequently, "We shall soon make their work easy" (8). This is the Quranic hero. In contrast, the bad people are miserly, forgetful and the deniers of truth. For such a wretch, "We shall make his work hard" (10).

Surat Al-Duha [93] - The Morning Brightness

This Surat was revealed to reassure the Prophet ﷺ. After a long pause in a revelation, he is given a four-point strategy to overcome stress and sorrow: get rid of negative thoughts, be determined that you will succeed, recall your past successes and set yourself clear targets. The powerful message it contains is an amazing force field of energy which, can heal our anxieties.

Surat Al-Inshirah [94] - The Expansion

This Surat builds on the previous Surat's consolation of the Messenger ﷺ in an affectionate tone. The opening or the expansion of the chest of the Prophet ﷺ was a miracle that prepared him to be the receptacle of Divine Revelation. It expresses the incredibly elevated position of the Messenger ﷺ.

Surat Al-Tin [95] - The Fig

This Surat opens with four oaths of valuable trees and sacred places, splendid symbols, testimony to the truthfulness of its theme: the 'inherent goodness' of human nature, and how easily it can be tarnished. The reference to human nature being as the "most beautiful" (4), offers hope in a world ravaged by wars and human greed. But this "most beautiful" nature can be easily damaged. The concept of Judgement Day acts as a deterrent.

Surat Al-'Alaq [96] - The Clot of Blood

This Surat was revealed in the cave of Hira. Here, in the stillness of the Mountain of Light, the Messenger ﷺ reflected on the waywardness of the Makkans. He loathed their idolatry, corrupt business practices and uncaring behaviour towards the poor. It was during a retreat that the Holy Spirit, Jibreel brought this first revelation.

Surat Al-Qadr [97] - The Night of Destiny

This Surat commends the night on which the Majestic Quran was revealed. A night in the month of Ramadan when the Quran was transferred from the Protected Tablet in the upper heaven to the lower heaven. Then gradually revealed to the Messenger ﷺ over a period of twenty-three years. The angels, human destiny and peace descend this night.

Surat Al-Bayyinah [98] - The Clear Proof

This Surat deals with the scepticism, resistance and disbelief of the idolaters, Jews and Christians. The Surat seeks to console the Prophet ﷺ and his followers that they need not be disappointed at such rejection.

Surat Al-Zilzal [99] - The Earthquake

This Surat talks of accountability on the Day of Resurrection. An earthquake will flatten the earth; mountains will turn to rubble, the seas will surge and the Earth will reveal its secrets. Yet the mindless person will have spent an entire life without a thought for the Hereafter. An authoritative reminder that on Judgement Day you must give an account.

Surat Al-'Adiyat [100] - The War Horses

This Surat describes the unthankful nature of humans. The word Kufr, a key theme in the Quran. A Kafir is an unthankful person, who fails to acknowledge the gifts of the Generous Lord. Hell is the only place that will cleanse humanity of this sin.

Surat Al-Qari'ah [101] - The Sudden Calamity

This Surat asks a question about Judgement Day in order to open our eyes to its reality. Then describes its momentous events. The root of a successful life is good deeds and those who lack good deeds will have "a blazing fire" (11).

Surat Al-Takathur [102] - The competition for More and More

This Surat highlights human greed for material things. It attempts to shock us in order to awaken our spiritual faculties and make us appreciate that material wealth cannot save us from death. So, we must accept the Hereafter.

Surat Al-Asr [103] - The Age

This Surat has a pithy message: life is short and fleeting, so save yourself by believing, doing good works, be truthful and patient.

Surat Al-Humazah [104] - The Faultfinder

This Surat condemns those with a negative attitude towards others, who continually search for faults and are obsessed with wealth. Hell is the only fitting place for them.

Surat Al-Fil [105] - The Elephant

This Surat reminds us of how Allah takes care of his people and places. Abraha's mighty army couldn't harm Makkah or the sacred Kaaba. The Surat hints to the protective power of Allah.

Surat Al-Quraysh [106] - The Tribe of Quraysh

This Surat highlights Allah's favours: provision of our livelihood, security from danger.

Surat Al-Ma'un [107] - Small Kindness

This Surat describes the person who is self-centred and heartless. He is incapable of even 'small kindnesses'. He shows no concern for the needy and won't even share his cooking pot! His worship is mere show.

Surat Al-Kawthar [108] - The Abundance

This Surat is a masterpiece of eloquence and such a morale booster. You have so much to thank Allah for, so pray and make the sacrifice. The enemy can not harm you.

Surat Al-Kafirun [109] - The Disbelievers

This Surat teaches us to 'never compromise our principles' but accept differences of religion and freedom of speech wholeheartedly.

Surat Al-Nasr [110] - The help

This Surat forecasts the Prophet's ﷺ mission is accomplished, victory imminent and hints to his demise.

Surat Al-Lahab [111] - The Flames

This Surat condemns Abu Lahab and his wife for insulting the Prophet ﷺ. Clearly showing that we must stand up for the truthful teachers and challenge their detractors.

Surat Al-Ikhlas [112] - Sincere Faith

This Surat defines Tawhid, the oneness of Allah, the eternal, no one is like Him.

Surat Al-Falaq [113] - The Daybreak

This Surat is an antidote to the sources of physical and psychic harm. Allah will protect you from the harm of creatures, invisible dark forces, magic and jealousy.

Surat Al-Nas [114] - The People

This Surat teaches us to seek Allah's protection against Satan.